# CHRISTIAN MISSIONS

# CHRISTIAN MISSIONS

## THEIR PLACE IN INDIA

**BY**

**M.K.GANDHI**

**Edited by**

**BHARATHAN KUMARAPPA**

GYAN

*Published by*

Gyan Publishing House
5, Ansari Road
Daryaganj, New Delhi-110002
Phone: 011-47034999, 9811692060
E-mail: books@gyanbooks.com

*Distribution Network*
gyanbooks.com
India, USA, Canada, UK, Australia



ISBN: 978-81-212-5524-0 (HB)
First Published, 1941

2nd Impression 2024

*Printed at:* Gyan Press, Delhi.



**CHRISTIAN MISSIONS**
Author: M.K.GANDHI, Editor: BHARATHAN KUMARAPPA

# CHRISTIAN MISSIONS

## THEIR PLACE IN INDIA

By

M. K. GANDHI

Edited by

BHARATAN KUMARAPPA

## PUBLISHER'S NOTE TO THE FIRST EDITION

The present volume makes another addition to the series of publications, undertaken by the Navajivan Press, containing collections of Gandhiji's writings and utterances on the many and varied subjects that he has dealt with, through *Young India* and *Harijan,* during the last twenty years. The present collection, though dealing with Christian Missions in particular, contains a few initial chapters that deal with the larger question of the equality of religions and thus provide the necessary background for the ideas propounded in the subsequent chapters. May the study of these contribute towards a better understanding between followers of different faiths, and goodwill and harmony among the warring creeds of the world. It is our hope that this volume will meet with the same enthusiastic welcome from the public as its forerunners have done.

1-3-1941

## EDITOR'S NOTE TO THE SECOND EDITION

The first edition of this book appeared in 1941. In this second edition the matter has been brought up to January 1948, when Gandhiji's life came to an end. The first edition had some writings bearing on the larger issue of equality of religions. As this topic has been covered adequately by other volumes issued since then, in this edition only such writings as relate to Christianity in India have been retained. The matter has also been slightly re-arranged.

Bharatan Kumarappa

## CONTENTS

## PART II

### Reports of Speeches And Conversations

*By Mahadev Desai*

*By Pyarelal*



*By Amrit Kaur*



*By Chandrashankar Shukla*



*A Post-Prayer Speech*

# CHRISTIAN MISSIONS

THEIR PLACE IN INDIA

## PART I

## GANDHIJI'S WRITINGS AND UTTERANCES

1

## GLIMPSES OF RELIGION

In Rajkot I got an early grounding in toleration for all branches of Hinduism and sister religions. For my father and mother would visit the *Haveli* as also Shiva's and Rama's temples, and would take or send us youngsters there. Jain monks also would pay frequent visits to my father, and would even go out of their way to accept food from us non-Jains. They would have talks with my father on subjects religious and mundane.

He had besides Mussalman and Parsi friends, who would talk to him about their own faiths, and he would listen to them always with respect, and often with interest. Being his nurse, I often had a chance to be present at these talks. These many things combined to inculcate in me a toleration for all faiths.

Only Christianity was at the time an exception. I developed a sort of dislike for it. And for a reason. In those days Christian missionaries used to stand in a corner near the High School and hold forth, pouring abuse on Hindus and their gods. I could not endure this. I must have stood there to hear them once only, but that was enough to dissuade me from repeating the experiment. About the same time, I heard of a well-known Hindu having been converted to Christianity. It was the talk of the town that, when he was baptized, he had to eat beef and drink liquor, that he also had to change his clothes, and that thenceforth he began to go about in European costume including a hat. These things got on my nerves. Surely, thought I, a religion that compelled one to eat beef, drink liquor, and change one's own clothes did not deserve the name. I also heard that the new convert had already begun abusing the religion of his ancestors, their customs and their country. All these things created in me a dislike for Christianity.

But one thing took deep root in me,—the conviction that morality is the basis of things, and that truth is the substance of all morality. Truth became my sole objective. It began to grow in magnitude everyday, and my definition of it also has been ever widening.

A Gujarati didactic stanza likewise gripped my mind and heart. Its precept,—return good for evil,—became my guiding principle. It became such a passion with me that I began numerous experiments in it. Here are those (for me) wonderful lines:

> For a bowl of water give a goodly meal;
> For a kindly greeting bow thou down with zeal;
> For a simple penny pay thou back with gold;
> If thy life be rescued, life do not withhold.
> Thus the words and actions of the wise regard;
> Every little service tenfold they reward.
> But the truly noble know all men as one,
> And return with gladness good for evil done.

*The Story of My Experiments with Truth,* Part I, Chap. X.

## 2

# A REPUDIATION

Rev. H. R. Scott at present stationed at Surat writes:

"I am specially interested in your account of those early days in Rajkot, because my first 14 years in India were spent in Kathiawad, one year in Gogha and 13 years in Rajkot. I was the only missionary in Rajkot during those years (from 1883 to 1897), and what you say about Christian missionaries in Rajkot standing at a corner near the High School and pouring abuse on Hindus and their gods fills me with a painful wonder. I certainly never preached 'at a corner near the High School'; my regular preaching station was under a banyan tree in the Para Bazar; and I certainly never 'poured abuse on Hindus and their gods'. That would be a strange way to win a hearing from Hindus. Then you say that a well-known Hindu was baptized at that time, and that 'he had to eat beef and drink liquor, and to change his clothes and go about in European costume, including a hat.' No wonder such a story got on your nerves, if you believed it. Well, I have been over 42 years in India, and I have never heard of such a thing happening; and indeed I know it to be quite contrary to what all missionaries with whom I am acquainted teach and believe and practise. During my time in Rajkot I baptized a number of Brahmins and Jain Sadhus. They certainly had not to 'eat beef and drink liquor', either at their baptism or at any other time. I have eaten beef myself of course as a European but I have never drunk liquor in my life. As I know, none of the Brahmins and Jains who were baptized by me in Rajkot ever ate beef or drank liquor. I know of course that this kind of story is told about converts to Christianity in Kathiawad and elsewhere in India. It is obviously the wilful invention of people who wish to prevent the spread of Christianity in India and hope thereby to frighten young Hindus who show an inclination to learn the truth about Christianity, and no doubt it has had its result in deterring many such honest inquirers as yourself. But surely you must have had many opportunities since then of discovering that that particular libel is without foundation, and as a sincere lover of truth you cannot wish to lend the great weight of your authority to perpetuate such a wilfully malicious misrepresentation of Christian missionaries. Please forgive me for writing so strongly, and for troubling you at all in the matter; but as many of my Hindu friends who know that I was the missionary at Rajkot during those years might not unreasonably suppose that you refer to me, I am sure that you will do what you can to make it clear that this is not so."

Though the preaching took place over forty years ago the painful memory of it is still vivid before me. What I have heard and read since has but confirmed that first impression. I have read several missionary publications, and they are able to see only the dark side and paint it darker still. The famous hymn of Bishop Heber's — "Greeland's icy mountains" — is a clear libel on Indian humanity. I was favoured with some literature even at the Yeravda prison by well-meaning missionaries which seemed to be written as if merely to belittle Hinduism. About beef-eating and wine-drinking at baptism I have merely stated what I heard and I have said as much in my writing. And whilst I accept Mr. Scott's repudiation I must say that, though I have mixed freely among thousands of Christian Indians, I know very few who have scruples about eating beef or other flesh meats and drinking intoxicating liquors. When I have gently reasoned with them, they have quoted to me the celebrated verse 'call thou nothing unclean' as if it referred to eating and gave a licence for indulgence. I know that many Hindus eat meat, some eat even beef and drink wines. They are not converts. Converts are those who are 'born again' or should be. A higher standard is expected of those who change their faith, if the change is a matter of the heart and not of convenience. But I must not enter into deeper waters. It is a matter of pleasure to me to be able to say that, if I have had painful experiences of Christians and Christian missionaries I have pleasant ones also which I treasure. There is no doubt that among them the spirit of toleration is growing. Among individuals there is also a deeper study of Hinduism and other faiths and an appreciation of their beauties, and among some even an admission that the other great faiths of the world are not false. One is thankful for the growing liberal spirit, but I have the conviction that much still remains to be done in that direction.

*Young India*, 4-3-'26

## 3

## ACQUAINTANCE WITH RELIGIONS

Towards the end of my second year in England I met a good Christian from Manchester in a vegetarian boarding house. He talked to me about Christianity. I narrated to him my Rajkot recollections. He was pained to hear them. He said, 'I am a vegetarian, I do not drink. Many Christians are meat-eaters and drink, no doubt; but neither meat-eating nor drinking is enjoined by Scripture. Do please read the Bible.' I accepted his advice and he got me a copy. I have a faint recollection that he himself used to sell copies of the Bible, and I purchased from him an edition containing maps, concordance, and other aids. I began reading it, but I could not possibly read through the Old Testament. I read the book of Genesis, and the chapters that followed invariably sent me to sleep. But just for the sake of being able to say that I had read it, I plodded through the other books with much difficulty and without the least interest or understanding. I disliked reading the book of Numbers.

But the New Testament produced a different impression, especially the Sermon on the Mount which went straight to my heart. I compared it with the *Gita*. The verses, 'But I say unto you, that ye resist not evil: but whosoever shall smite thee on thy right cheek, turn to him the other also. And if any man take away thy coat let him have thy cloak too,' delighted me beyond measure and put me in mind of Shamal Bhatt's 'For a bowl of water, give a goodly meal' etc.

*The Story of My Experiments with Truth*, Part I, Chap. XX.

## 4

## CHRISTIAN CONTACTS

The next day at one o'clock I went to Mr. Baker's prayer-meeting. There I was introduced to Miss Harris, Miss Gabb, Mr. Coates and others. Everyone kneeled down to pray and I followed suit. The prayers were supplications to God for various things, according to each person's desire. Thus the usual forms were for the day to be passed peacefully, or for God to open the doors of the heart.

A prayer was now added for my welfare: 'Lord, show the path to the new brother, who has come amongst us. Give him, Lord, the peace that Thou hast given us. May the Lord Jesus who has saved us save him too. We ask all this in the name of Jesus.' There was no singing of hymns or other music at these meetings. After the supplication for something special every day, we dispersed, each going to his lunch, that being the hour for it. The prayer did not take more than five minutes.

The Misses Harris and Gabb were both elderly maiden ladies. Mr. Coates was a Quaker. The two ladies lived together, and they gave me a standing invitation to four o'clock tea, at their house, every Sunday.

When we met on Sundays, I used to give Mr. Coates my religious diary for the week, and discuss with him the books I had read and the impression they had left on me. The ladies used to narrate their sweet experiences, and talk about the peace they had found.

Mr. Coates was a frank-hearted staunch young man. We went out for walks together, and he also took me to other Christian friends.

As we came closer to each other, he began to give me books of his own choice, until my shelf was filled with them. He loaded me with books, as it were. In pure faith I consented to read all those books, and as I went on reading them, we discussed them.

I read a number of such books in 1893. I do not remember the names of them all, but they included the *Commentary* of Dr. Parker of the City Temple, Pearson's *Many Infallible Proofs* and Butler's *Analogy*. Parts of these were unintelligible to me. I liked some things in them, while I did not like others. *Many Infallible Proofs* were proofs in support of the religion of the Bible as the author understood it. The book had no effect on me. Parker's *Commentary* was morally stimulating, but it could not be of any help to one who had no faith in the prevalent Christian beliefs. Butler's *Analogy* struck me to be a very profound and difficult book, which should be read four or five times to be understood properly. It seemed to me to be written with a view to converting atheists to theism. The arguments advanced in it regarding the existence of God were unnecessary for me, as I had then passed the stage of unbelief; but the arguments in proof of Jesus being the only incarnation of God and the Mediator between God and man left me unmoved.

But Mr. Coates was not the man easily to accept defeat. He had great affection for me. He saw, round my neck, the *Vaishnava* necklace of Tulasi-beads. He thought it to be superstition, and was pained by it. 'This superstition does not become you. Come, let me break the necklace.'

'No, you will not. It is a sacred gift from my mother.'

'But do you believe in it?'

'I do not know its mysterious significance. I do not think I should come to harm if I did not wear it. But I cannot, without sufficient reason, give up a necklace that she put round my neck out of love and in the conviction that it would be conducive to my welfare. When, with the passage of time, it wears away and breaks of its own accord, I shall have no desire to get a new one. But this necklace cannot be broken.'

Mr. Coates could not appreciate my argument, as he had no regard for my religion. He was looking forward to delivering me from the abyss of ignorance. He wanted to convince me that, no matter whether there was some truth in other religions, salvation was impossible for me unless I accepted Christianity which represented *the* truth, and that my sins would not be washed away except by the intercession of Jesus, and that all good works were useless.

Just as he introduced me to several books, he introduced me to several friends whom he regarded as staunch Christians. One of these introductions was to a family which belonged to the Plymouth Brethren, a Christian sect.

Many of the contacts for which Mr. Coates was responsible were good. Most struck me as being God-fearing. But during my contact with this family, one of the Plymouth Brethren confronted me with an argument for which I was not prepared:

'You cannot understand the beauty of our religion. From what you say it appears that you must be brooding over your transgressions every moment of your life, always mending them and atoning for them. How can this ceaseless cycle of action bring you redemption? You can never have peace. You admit that we are all sinners. Now look at the perfection of our belief. Our attempts at improvement and atonement are futile. And yet redemption we must have. How can we bear the burden of sin? We can but throw it on Jesus. He is the only sinless Son of God. It is His word that those who believe in Him shall have everlasting life. Therein lies God's infinite mercy. And as we believe in the atonement of Jesus, our own sins do not bind us. Sin we must. It is impossible to live in this world sinless. And therefore Jesus suffered and atoned for all the sins of mankind. Only he who accepts His great redemption can have eternal peace. Think what a life of restlessness is yours, and what a promise of peace we have.'

The argument utterly failed to convince me. I humbly replied:

'If this be the Christianity acknowledged by all Christians, I cannot accept it. I do not seek redemption from the consequences of my sin. I seek to be redeemed from sin itself, or rather from the very thought of sin. Until I have attained that end, I shall be content to be restless.'

To which the Plymouth Brother rejoined: 'I assure you, your attempt is fruitless. Think again over what I have said.'

And the Brother proved as good as his word. He knowingly committed transgressions and showed me that he was undisturbed by the thought of them.

But I already knew before meeting with these friends, that all Christians did not believe in such a theory of atonement. Mr. Coates himself walked in the fear of God. His heart was pure, and he believed in the possibility of self-purification. The two ladies also shared this belief. Some of the books that came into my hands were full of devotion. So although Mr. Coates was very much disturbed by this latest experience of mine, I was able to reassure him and tell him that the distorted belief of a Plymouth Brother could not prejudice me against Christianity.

My difficulties lay elsewhere. They were with regard to the Bible and its accepted interpretation.

*The Story of My Experiments with Truth,* Part II, Chap. XI.

## 5

## RELIGIOUS FERMENT

Mr. Baker was getting anxious about my future. He took me to the Wellington Convention. The Protestant Christians organize such gatherings every few years for religious enlightenment or, in other words, self-purification. One may call this religious restoration or revival. The Wellington Convention was of this type. The chairman was the famous divine of the place, the Rev. Andrew Murray. Mr. Baker had hoped that the atmosphere of religious exaltation at the Convention, and the enthusiasm and earnestness of the people attending it would inevitably lead me to embrace Christianity.

But his final hope was the efficacy of prayer. He had an abiding faith in prayer. It was his firm conviction that God could not but listen to prayer fervently offered. He would cite the instances of men like George Muller of Bristol, who depended entirely on prayer even for his temporal needs. I listened to his discourse on the efficacy of prayer with unbiassed attention, and assured him that nothing could prevent me from embracing Christianity, should I feel the call. I had no hesitation in giving him this assurance, as I had long since taught myself to follow the inner voice. I delighted in submitting to it. To act against it would be difficult and painful to me.

So we went to Wellington.

This Convention was an assemblage of devout Christians. I was delighted at their faith. I met the Rev. Murray. I saw that many were praying for me. I liked some of their hymns, they were very sweet.

The Convention lasted for three days. I could understand and appreciate the devoutness of those who attended it. But I saw no reason for changing my belief — my religion. It was impossible for me to believe that I could go to heaven or attain salvation only by becoming a Christian. When I frankly said so to some of the good Christian friends, they were shocked. But there was no help for it.

My difficulties lay deeper. It was more than I could believe that Jesus was the only incarnate son of God, and that only he who believed in Him would have everlasting life. If God could have sons, all of us were his sons. If Jesus was like God, or God Himself, then all men were like God and could be God Himself. My reason was not ready to believe literally that Jesus by his death and by his blood redeemed the sins of the world. Metaphorically there might be some truth in it. Again, according to Christianity only human beings had souls, and not other living beings, for whom death meant complete extinction; while I held a contrary belief. I could accept Jesus as a martyr, an embodiment of sacrifice, and a divine teacher, but not as the most perfect man ever born. His death on the Cross was a great example to the world, but that there was anything like a mysterious or miraculous virtue in it, my heart could not accept. The pious lives of Christians did not give me anything that the lives of men of other faiths had failed to give. I had seen in other lives just the same reformation that I had heard of among Christians. Philosophically there was nothing extraordinary in Christian principles. From the point of view of sacrifice, it seemed to me that the Hindus greatly surpassed the Christians. It was impossible for me to regard Christianity as a perfect religion or the greatest of all religions.

I shared this mental churning with my Christian friends whenever there was an opportunity, but their answers could not satisfy me.

Thus if I could not accept Christianity either as a perfect, or the greatest, religion, neither was I then convinced of Hinduism being such. Hindu defects were pressingly visible to me. If untouchability could be a part of Hinduism, it could but be a rotten part or an excrescence. I could not understand the *raison d'etre* of a multitude of sects and castes. What was the meaning of saying that the Vedas were the inspired Word of God? If they were inspired, why not also the Bible and the Koran?

As Christian friends were endeavouring to convert me, even so were Mussalman friends. Abdulla Sheth had kept on inducing me to study Islam, and of course he had always something to say regarding its beauty.

I expressed my difficulties in a letter to Raychandbhai. I also corresponded with other religious authorities in India and received answers from them. Raychandbhai's letter somewhat pacified me. He asked me to be patient and to study Hinduism more deeply. One of his sentences was to this effect: 'On a dispassionate view of the question, I am convinced that no other religion has the subtle and profound thought of Hinduism, its vision of the soul, or its charity.'

I purchased Sale's translation of the Koran and began reading it. I also obtained other books on Islam. I communicated with Christian friends in England. One of them introduced me to Edward Maitland, with whom I opened correspondence. He sent me *The Perfect Way*, a book he had written in collaboration with Anna Kingsford. The book was a repudiation of the current Christian belief. He also sent me another book, *The New Interpretation of the Bible*. I liked both. They seemed to support Hinduism. Tolstoy's *The Kingdom of God is within You* overwhelmed me. It left an abiding impression on me. Before the independent thinking, profound morality, and the truthfulness of this book, all the books given me by Mr. Coates seemed to pale into insignificance.

My studies thus carried me in a direction unthought of by the Christian friends. My correspondence with Edward Maitland was fairly prolonged, and that with Raychandbhai continued until his death. I read some of the books he sent me. These included *Panchikaran, Maniratnamala, Mumukshu Prakaran* of *Yogavasishtha,* Haribhadra Suri's *Shaddarshana Samuchchaya* and others.

Though I took a path my Christian friends had not intended for me, I have remained for ever indebted to them for the religious quest that they awakened in me. I shall always cherish the memory of their contact. The years that followed had more, not less, of such sweet and sacred contacts in store for me.

*The Story of My Experiments with Truth,* Part II, Chap. XV.

## 6

## COMPARATIVE STUDY OF RELIGIONS

Christian friends had whetted my appetite for knowledge which had become almost insatiable, and they would not leave me in peace, even if I desired to be indifferent. In Durban Mr. Spencer Walton, the head of the South Africa General Mission, found me out. I became almost a member of his family. At the back of this acquaintance was of course my contact with Christians in Pretoria. Mr. Walton had a manner all his own. I do not recollect his ever having invited me to embrace Christianity. But he placed his life as an open book before me, and let me watch all his movements. Mrs. Walton was a very gentle and talented woman. I liked the attitude of this couple. We knew the fundamental differences between us. Any amount of discussion could not efface them. Yet even differences prove helpful, where there are tolerance, charity and truth. I liked Mr. and Mrs. Walton's humility, perseverance and devotion to work, and we met very frequently.

This friendship kept alive my interest in religion. It was impossible now to get the leisure that I used to have in Pretoria for my religious studies. But what little time I could spare I turned to good account. My religious correspondence continued. Raychandbhai was guiding me. Some friend sent me Narmadashankar's book *Dharma Vichar*. Its preface proved very helpful. I had heard about the Bohemian way in which the poet had lived, and a description, in the preface, of the revolution effected in his life by his religious studies captivated me. I came to like the book, and read it from cover to cover with attention. I read with interest Max Muller's book, *India—What can It Teach Us*? and the translation of the *Upanishads* published by the Theosophical Society. All this enhanced my regard for Hinduism, and its beauties began to grow upon me. It did not, however, prejudice me against other religions. I read Washington Irving's *Life of Mahomet and His Successors* and Carlyle's panegyric on the Prophet. These books raised Muhammad in my estimation. I also read a book called *The Sayings of Zarathustra*.

Thus I gained more knowledge of the different religions. The study stimulated my self-introspection, and fostered in me the habit of putting into practice whatever appealed to me in my studies. Thus I began some of the Yogic practices, as well as I could understand them from a reading of the Hindu books. But I could not get on very far, and decided to follow them with the help of some expert when I returned to India. The desire has never been fulfilled.

I made too an intensive study of Tolstoy's books. *The Gospels in Brief*, *What to Do*?, and other books made a deep impression on me. I began to realize more and more the infinite possibilities of universal love.

About the same time I came in contact with another Christian family. At their suggestion, I attended the Wesleyan Church every Sunday. For these days I also had their standing invitation to dinner. The church did not make a favourable impression on me. The sermons seemed to be uninspiring. The congregation did not strike me as being particularly religious. They were not an assembly of devout souls; they appeared rather to be worldly-minded people going to church for recreation and in conformity to custom. Here, at times, I would involuntarily doze. I was ashamed, but some of my neighbours, who were in no better case, lightened the shame. I could not go on long like this, and soon gave up attending the service.

My connection with the family I used to visit every Sunday was abruptly broken. In fact it may be said that I was warned to visit it no more. It happened thus. My hostess was a good and simple woman, but somewhat narrow-minded. We always discussed religious subjects. I was then re-reading Arnold's *Light of Asia.* Once we began to compare the life of Jesus with that of Buddha. 'Look at Gautama's compassion!' said I. 'It was not confined to mankind, it was extended to all living beings. Does not one's heart overflow with love to think of the lamb joyously perched on his shoulders? One fails to notice this love for all living beings in the life of Jesus.' The comparison pained the good lady. I could understand her feelings. I cut the matter short, and we went to the dining room. Her son, a cherub aged scarcely five, was also with us. I am happiest when in the midst of children, and this youngster and I had long been friends. I spoke derisively of the piece of meat on his plate and in high praise of the apple on mine. The innocent boy was carried away and joined in my praise of the fruit.

But the mother? She was dismayed. I was warned. I checked myself and changed the subject. The following week I visited the family as usual, but not without trepidation. I did not see that I should stop going there, I did not think it proper either. But the good lady made my way easy.

'Mr. Gandhi,' she said, 'please don't take it ill if I feel obliged to tell you that my boy is none the better for your company. Every day he hesitates to eat meat and asks for fruit, reminding me of your argument. This is too much. If he gives up meat, he is bound to get weak, if not ill. How could I bear it? Your discussions should henceforth be only with us elders. They are sure to react badly on children.'

'Mrs.—,' I replied, 'I am sorry. I can understand your feelings as a parent, for I too have children. We can very easily end this unpleasant state of things. What I eat and omit to eat is bound to have a greater effect on the child than what I say. The best way, therefore, is for me to stop these visits. That certainly need not affect our friendship.'

'I thank you,' she said with evident relief.

*The Story of My Experiments with Truth*, Part II, Chap. XXII.

## 7

## EQUALITY OF RELIGIONS

### I

If we are imperfect ourselves, religion as conceived by us must also be imperfect. We have not realized religion in its perfection, even as we have not realized God. Religion of our conception, being thus imperfect, is always subject to a process of evolution and re-interpretation. Progress towards Truth, towards God, is possible only because of such evolution. And if all faiths outlined by men are imperfect, the question of comparative merit does not arise. All faiths constitute a revelation of Truth, but all are imperfect, and liable to error. Reverence for other faiths need not blind us to their faults. We must be keenly alive to the defects of our own faith also, yet not leave it on that account, but try to overcome those defects. Looking at all religions with an equal eye, we would not only not hesitate, but would think it our duty, to blend into our faith every acceptable feature of other faiths.

II

My meaning will perhaps become clearer, if I describe here some of my experiences. In Phoenix we had our daily prayers in the same way as in Sabarmati, and Mussalmans as well as Christians attended them along with Hindus. The late Sheth Rustomji and his children too frequented the prayer meetings. Rustomji Sheth very much liked the Gujarati *bhajan*, '*Mane valun*', 'Dear, dear to me is the name of Rama'. If my memory serves me right, Maganlal or Kashi was once leading us in singing this hymn, when Rustomji Sheth exclaimed joyously, 'Say the name of Hormazd instead of the name of Rama.' His suggestion was readily taken up, and after that whenever the Sheth was present, and sometimes even when he was not, we put in the name of Hormazd in place of Rama. The late Husain, son of Daud Sheth, often stayed at the Phoenix Ashram, and enthusiastically joined our prayers. To the accompaniment of an organ, he used to sing in a very sweet voice the song '*Hai bahare bag*', 'The garden of this world has only a momentary bloom.' He taught us all this song, which we also sang at prayers. Its inclusion in our *Bhajanavali** is a tribute to truth-loving Husain's memory. I have never met a young man who practised Truth more devotedly than Husain. Joseph Royeppen often came to Phoenix. He is a Christian, and his favourite hymn was '*Vaishnava jana*', 'He is a *Vaishnava* (servant of the Lord), who succours people in distress.' He loved music and once sang this hymn, saying 'Christian' in the place of *Vaishnava*. The others accepted his reading with alacrity, and I observed that this filled Joseph's heart with joy.

When I was turning over the pages of the sacred books of different faiths for my own satisfaction, I became sufficiently familiar for my purpose with Christianity, Islam, Zoroastrianism, Judaism and Hinduism. In reading these

* Published by the Navajivan Publishing House, Ahmedabad-14.

texts, I can say, I was equiminded towards all these faiths, although perhaps I was not then conscious of it. Refreshing my memory of those days, I do not find I ever had the slightest desire to criticize any of those religions merely because they were not my own, but read each sacred book in a spirit of reverence, and found the same fundamental morality in each. Some things I did not understand then, and do not understand even now, but experience has taught me that it is a mistake hastily to imagine that anything that we cannot understand is necessarily wrong. Some things which I did not understand first have since become as clear as daylight. Equimindedness helps us to solve many difficulties and even when we criticize anything, we express ourselves with a humility and a courtesy which leave no sting behind them.

The acceptance of the doctrine of Equality of Religions does not abolish the distinction between religion and irreligion. We do not propose to cultivate toleration for irreligion. That being so, some people might object that there would be no room left for equimindedness, if every one took his own decision as to what was religion and what was irreligion. If we follow the law of Love, we shall not bear any hatred towards the irreligious brother. On the contrary, we shall love him, and therefore either we shall bring him to see the error of his ways, or he will point out our error, or each will tolerate the other's difference of opinion. If the other party does not observe the law of Love, he may be violent to us. If, however, we cherish real love for him, it will overcome his bitterness in the end. All obstacles in our path will vanish, if only we observe the golden rule that we must not be impatient with those whom we may consider to be in error, but must be prepared, if need be, to suffer in our own person.

*From Yeravda Mandir,* Chap. X & XI.

The need of the moment is not one religion, but mutual respect and tolerance of the devotees of the different religions. We want to reach not the dead level, but unity in diversity. Any attempt to root out traditions, effects of heredity, climate and other surroundings is not only bound to fail but is a sacrilege. The soul of religions is one, but it is encased in a multitude of forms. The latter will persist to the end of time. Wise men will ignore the outward crust and see the same soul living under a variety of crusts. For Hindus to expect Islam, Christianity or Zoroastrianism to be driven out of India is as idle a dream as it would be for Mussalmans to have only Islam of their imagination rule the world. But if belief in One God and the race of His Prophet in a never-ending chain is sufficient for Islam, then we are all Mussalmans, but we are also all Hindus and Christians. Truth is the exclusive property of no single scripture.

*Young India*, 25-9-'24

8

## NEED FOR TOLERANCE

A Mussalman friend has addressed me a long letter of which the following is the gist:

> "I turned a vegetarian several years ago, being struck by the iniquitous cruelty of slaughtering God's dumb creatures to provide meat for our tables. Ever since then I have completely abjured the taking of meat though meat-eating is allowed by Islam. But I have not been able to induce my children to abjure meat-eating likewise, with the result that I have still to procure meat for them from the bazaar. Sometimes, however, I am troubled by a doubt whether this is not all wrong. Would I remain a silent witness, if my children took to theft and murder, for instance? Would I not in that case exhaust all efforts to wean them from their career of crime, and, if they failed, even to invoke the law against them and hand them over to the authorities? And would I be guilty of violence if I did that? How far, then, is it compatible with right and justice to cause innocent animals to be slaughtered from day to day in order to cater for my family?

> You regard Mahomed as a Prophet of God and hold him in high regard. You have even publicly spoken of him in the highest terms. I have heard and even seen reports in cold print to the effect that you have studied the Koran itself. All this, I must confess, has puzzled me. I am at a loss to understand how a person like you, with all your passion for truth and justice, who has never failed to gloze over a single fault in Hinduism or to repudiate as unauthentic the numerous corruptions that masquerade under it, can holus-bolus accept all that is in the Koran. I am not aware of your ever having called into question or denounced any iniquitous injunction of Islam. Against some of these I learnt to revolt when I was scarcely 18 or 20 years old, and time has since only strengthened that first feeling."

I have tried as far as was possible to retain the language of the original, taking liberty only to soften a few expressions here and there, but have otherwise scrupulously kept the sense intact. To come to the various points mentioned by my correspondent. He deserves to be congratulated on his giving up meat-eating and on the various other disciplines that he has cultivated. But he may not impose the same on his unwilling or half-willing relations or dependants. Let him try to touch their hearts and reason by all the means of persuasion at his command; but anything more than that before the desired conversion has come about, would be compulsion and therefore unjustifiable. It would obviously be too much for him to expect the members of his family, all of a sudden, to break with a life-long habit that has never been regarded as contrary to Islam, which is almost universal among the Mussalmans today and till yesterday was followed by the friend in question himself. Let him not forget the long years of strenuous introspection and struggle which he took before he arrived at his decision. To require now his dependants to adopt that decision at a stroke would only betray impatience on his part. The golden rule to be observed always in this connection is that you can never be too severe in dealing with yourself but you must be deliberately liberal in judging others. For, experience has shown that, no matter how severe we may try to be with regard to ourselves, we shall, in the result, still be found to have acted partially towards ourselves, for the simple reason that our unconscious bias always prepossesses us in our favour and seldom allows the test to be carried beyond our capacity for endurance. But in the case of others we do not know their weaknesses and limitations, which are known only to God who alone can read our hearts. There is therefore always a danger, with all our desire to be liberal, of our being betrayed into a hollow harshness and intolerance when we proceed to apply our personal standards to others; and paradoxical though it may sound, the more liberal, the more patient, the more considerate we are in such cases, the quicker the results are likely to be; they will certainly be more permanent and lasting.

The analogy between meat-eating and theft or murder drawn by the correspondent in question is altogether untenable. Theft and murder, unlike meat-eating, are universally held to be crimes and are heavily punishable under the law. But even so one may not, in the hypothetical case cited above, try to wean dependants and relations from their career of theft and murder through compulsion. My correspondent must, therefore, try to convert members of his household to his view by patient argument alone, tempered by love, and pending their conversion, cultivate an attitude of the broadest tolerance and forbearance towards them.

Now for Islam. I stand by every word that I have written in that connection. I have nowhere said that I believe literally in every word of the Koran, or for the matter of that of any scripture in the world. But it is no business of mine to criticize the scriptures of other faiths, or to point out their defects. It is and should be, however, my privilege to proclaim and practise the truths that there may be in them. I may not, therefore, criticize or condemn things in the Koran or the life of the Prophet that I cannot understand. But I welcome every opportunity to express my admiration for such aspects of his life as I have been able to appreciate and understand. As for things that present difficulties, I am content to see them through the eyes of devout Mussalman friends, while I try to understand them with the help of the writings of eminent Muslim expounders of Islam. It is only through such a reverential approach to faiths other than mine that I can realize the principle of equality of all religions. But it is both my right and duty to point out the defects in Hinduism in order to purify it and to keep it pure. But when non-Hindu critics set about criticizing Hinduism and cataloguing its faults they only blazon their own ignorance of Hinduism and their incapacity to regard it from the Hindu viewpoint. It distorts their vision and vitiates their judgment. Thus my own experience of the non-Hindu critics of Hinduism brings home to me my limitations and teaches me to be wary of launching on a criticism of Islam or Christianity and their founders.

*Harijan*, 13-3-'37

## 9

## CRIME OF READING BIBLE

Several correspondents have written to me taking me to task for reading the New Testament to the students of the Gujarat National College. One of them asks:

> "Will you please say why you are reading the Bible to the students of the Gujarat National College? Is there nothing useful in our literature? Is the Gita less to you than the Bible? You are never tired of saying that you are a staunch Sanatani Hindu. Have you not now been found out as a Christian in secret? You may say a man does not become a Christian by reading the Bible. But is not reading

the Bible to the boys a way of converting them to Christianity? Can the boys remain uninfluenced by the Bible reading? Are they not likely to become Christians by reading the Bible? What is there specially in the Bible that is not to be found in our sacred books? I do hope you will give an adequate reply and give preference to the Vedas over the Bible."

I am afraid I cannot comply with the last request of my correspondent. I must give preference to that which the boys lawfully want over what I or others may desire. When they invited me to give them an hour per week, I gave them the choice between reading the Gita, Tulsidas' Ramayana, and answering questions. By a majority of votes, they decided to have the New Testament and questions and answers. In my opinion, the boys were entitled to make that choice. They have every right to read the Bible or to have it read to them. I offered to read the Gita or the Ramayana as I am reading both at the Ashram to the inmates and as therefore the reading of either at the National College would have involved the least strain and the least preparation. But the boys of the College probably thought they could read the other books through others but they would have from me my interpretation of the New Testament as they knew that I had made a fair study of it.

I hold that it is the duty of every cultured man or woman to read sympathetically the scriptures of the world. If we are to respect others' religions as we would have them to respect our own, a friendly study of the world's religions is a sacred duty. We need not dread, upon our grown up children, the influence of scriptures other than our own. We liberalize their outlook upon life by encouraging them to study freely all that is clean. Fear there would be when someone reads his own scriptures to young people with intention secretly or openly of converting them. He must then be biassed in favour of his own scriptures. For myself, I regard my study of and reverence for the Bible, the Koran, and the other scriptures to be wholly consistent with my claim to be a staunch Sanatani Hindu. He is no Sanatani Hindu who is narrow, bigoted, and considers evil to be good if it has the sanction of antiquity and is to be found supported in any Sanskrit book. I claim to be a staunch Sanatani Hindu because, though I reject all that offends my moral sense, I find the Hindu scriptures to satisfy the needs of the soul. My respectful study of other religions has not abated my reverence for or my faith in the Hindu scriptures. They have indeed left their deep mark upon my understanding of the Hindu scriptures. They have broadened my view of life. They have enabled me to understand more clearly many an obscure passage in the Hindu scriptures.

The charge of being a Christian in secret is not new. It is both a libel and a compliment—a libel because there are men who can believe me to be capable of being secretly anything, i.e. for fear of being that openly. There is nothing in the world that would keep me from professing Christianity or any other faith, the moment I felt the truth of and the need for it. Where there is fear there is no religion. The charge is a compliment in that it is a reluctant acknowledgement of my capacity for appreciating the beauties of Christianity. Let me own this. If I could call myself, say, a Christian or a Mussalman, with my own interpretation of the Bible or the Koran, I should not hesitate to call myself either. For then Hindu, Christian and Mussalman would be synonymous terms. I do believe that in the other world there are neither Hindus nor Christians nor Mussalmans. There all are judged not according to their labels or professions but according to their actions irrespective of their professions. During our earthly existence there will always be these labels. I therefore prefer to retain the label of my forefathers so long as it does not cramp my growth and does not debar me from assimilating all that is good anywhere else.

*Young India*, 2-9-'26

## 10

# WHY I AM A HINDU

An American friend who subscribes herself as a life-long friend of India writes:

> "As Hinduism is one of the prominent religions of the East, and as you have made a study of Christianity and Hinduism, and on the basis of that study have announced that you are a Hindu, I beg leave to ask of you if you will do me the favour to give me your reasons for that choice. Hindus and Christians alike realize that man's chief need is to know God and to worship Him in spirit and in truth. Believing that Christ was a revelation of God, Christians of America have sent to India thousands of their sons and daughters to tell the people of India about Christ. Will you in return kindly give us your interpretation of Hinduism and make a comparison of Hinduism with the teachings of Christ? I will be deeply grateful for this favour."

I have ventured at several missionary meetings to tell English and American missionaries that, if they could have refrained from 'telling' India about Christ and had merely lived a life enjoined upon them by the Sermon on the Mount, India instead of suspecting them would have appreciated their living in the midst of her children and directly profited by their presence. Holding this view, I can 'tell' American friends nothing about Hinduism by way of 'return'. I do not believe in people telling others of their faith, especially with a view to conversion. Faith does not admit of telling. It has to be lived and then it becomes self-propagating.

Nor do I consider myself fit to interpret Hinduism except through my own life. And if I may not interpret Hinduism through my written word, I may not compare it with Christianity. The only thing it is possible for me, therfore, to do is to say, as briefly as I can, why I am a Hindu.

Believing as I do in the influence of heredity, being born in a Hindu family, I have remained a Hindu. I should reject it, if I found it inconsistent with my moral sense or my spiritual growth. On examination I have found it to be the most tolerant of all religions known to me. Its freedom from dogma makes a forcible appeal to me inasmuch as it gives the votary the largest scope for self-expression. Not being an exclusive religion, it enables the followers of that faith not merely to respect all the other religions, but it also enables them to admire and assimilate whatever may be good in the other faiths. Non-violence is common to all religions, but it has found the highest expression and application in Hinduism. (I do not regard Jainism or Buddhism as separate from Hinduism.) Hinduism believes in the oneness not of merely all human life but in the oneness of all that lives. Its worship of the cow is, in my opinion, its unique contribution to the evolution of humanitarianism. It is a practical application of the belief in the oneness and, therefore, sacredness of all life. The great belief in transmigration is a direct consequence of that belief. Finally, the discovery of the law of Varnashrama is a magnificent result of the ceaseless search for truth. I must not burden this article with definitions of the essentials sketched here, except to say that the present ideas of cow worship and Varnashrama are a caricature of what in my opinion the originals are. The curious may see the definitions of cow worship and Varnashrama in the previous numbers of *Young India.* I hope to have to say on Varnashrama in the near future. In this all too brief a sketch I have mentioned what occur to me to be the outstanding features of Hinduism that keep me in its fold.

*Young India,* 20-10-'27

11

# AN ADDRESS TO MISSIONARIES

[I had the pleasure of delivering an address before the missionaries in Calcutta at Y. W. C. A. on 28th ultimo. I reproduce below an abridgement of it. —M. K. G.]

Not many of you perhaps know that my association with Christians—not Christians so-called but real Christians—dates from 1889 when as a lad I found myself in London; and that association has grown riper as years have rolled on. In South Africa where I found myself in the midst of inhospitable surroundings I was able to make hundreds of Christian friends. I came in touch with the late Mr. Spencer Watton, Director of South Africa General Mission, and later with the great divine Rev. Mr. A. Murray and several others.

My acquaintance, therefore, this evening with so many missionaries is by no means a new thing. There was even a time in my life when a very sincere and intimate friend of mine, a great and good Quaker, had designs on me (laughter). He thought that I was too good not to become a Christian. I was sorry to have disappointed him. One missionary friend of mine in South Africa still writes to me and asks me, 'How is it with you?' I have always told this friend that so far as I know it is all well with me. If it was prayer that these friends expected me to make, I was able to tell them that every day the heart-felt prayer within the closed door of my closet went to the Almighty to show me light and give wisdom and courage to follow that light.

In answer to promises made to one of these Christian friends of mine I thought it my duty to see one of the biggest of Indian Christians, as I was told he was,—the late Kali Charan Banerjee. I went over to him—I am telling you of the deep search that I have undergone in order that I might leave no stone unturned to find out the true path—I went to him with an absolutely open mind and in a receptive mood, and I met him also under circumstances which were most affecting. I found that there was much in common between Mr. Banerjee and myself. His simplicity, his humility, his courage, his truthfulness, all these things I have all along admired. He met me when his wife was on her death-bed. You cannot imagine a more impressive scene, a more ennobling circumstance. I told Mr. Banerjee, 'I have come to you as a seeker'—this was in 1901—'I have come to you in fulfilment of a sacred promise I have made to some of my dearest Christian friends that I will leave no stone unturned to find out the true light.' I told him that I had given my friends the assurance that no worldly gain would keep me away from the light, if I could but see it. Well, I am not going to engage you in giving a description of the little discussion that we had between us. It was very good, very noble. I came away, not sorry, not dejected, not disappointed, but I felt sad that even Mr. Banerjee could not convince me. This was my final deliberate striving to realize Christianity as it was presented to me. Today my position is that, though I admire much in Christianity, I am unable to identify myself with orthodox Christianity. I must tell you in all humility that Hinduism, as I know it, entirely satisfies my soul, fills my whole being, and I find a solace in the Bhagavadgita and Upanishads that I miss even in the Sermon on the Mount. Not that I do not prize the ideal presented therein, not that some of the precious teachings in the Sermon on the Mount have not left a deep impression upon me, but I must confess to you that when doubts haunt me, when disappointments stare me in the face, and when I see not one ray of light on the horizon I turn to the Bhagavadgita and find a verse to comfort me; and I immediately begin to smile in the midst of overwhelming sorrow. My life has been full of external tragedies and, if they have not left any visible and indelible effect on me, I owe it to the teaching of the Bhagavadgita.

I have told you all these things in order to make it absolutely clear to you where I stand, so that I may have, if you will, closer touch with you. I must add that I did not stop at studying the Bible and the commentaries and other books on Christianity that my friends placed in my hands; but I said to myself, if I was to find my satisfaction through reasoning, I must study the scriptures of other religions also and make my choice. And I turned to the Koran. I tried to understand what I could of Judaism as distinguished from Christianity. I studied Zoroastrianism and I came to the conclusion that all religions were right but every one of them was imperfect, imperfect naturally and necessarily, because they were interpreted with our poor intellects, sometimes with our poor hearts and more often misinterpreted. In all religions I found to my grief that there were various and even contradictory interpretations of some texts, and I said to myself, 'Not these things for me. If I want the satisfaction of my soul, I must feel my way. I must wait silently upon God and ask Him to guide me.' There is a beautiful verse in Sanskrit which says, 'God helps only when man feels utterly helpless and utterly humble.' Some of you have come from the Tamil land. When I was studying Tamil, I found in one of the books of Dr. Pope a Tamil proverb which means 'God helps the helpless.' I have given you this life-story of my own experience for you to ponder over.

You, the missionaries come to India thinking that you come to a land of heathens, of idolaters, of men who do not know God. One of the greatest of Christian divines, Bishop Heber, wrote the two lines which have always left a sting with me: 'Where every prospect pleases, and only man is vile.' I wish he had not written them. My own experience in my travels throughout India has been to the contrary. I have gone from one end of the country to the other, without any prejudice, in a relentless search after truth, and I am not able to say that here in this fair land, watered by the great Ganges, the Brahmaputra and the Jumna, man is vile, He is not vile. He is as much a seeker after truth as you and I are, possibly more so. This reminds me of a French book translated for me by a French friend. It is an account of an imaginary expedition in search of knowledge. One party landed in India and found Truth and God personified, in a little Pariah's hut. I tell you there are many such huts belonging to the untouchables where you will certainly find God. They do not reason, but they persist in their belief that God is. They depend upon God for His assistance and find it too. There are many stories told throughout the length and breadth of India about these noble untouchables. Vile as some of them may be there are noblest specimens of humanity in their midst. But does my experience exhaust itself merely with the untouchables? No, I am here to tell you that there are non-Brahmins, there are Brahmins who are as fine specimens of humanity as you will find in any place on the earth. There are Brahmins, today in India who are embodiments of self-sacrifice, godliness, and humility. There are Brahmins who are devoting themselves body and soul to the service of untouchables, with no expectation of reward from the untouchables, but with execration from orthodoxy. They do not mind it, because in serving Pariahs they are serving God. I can quote chapter and verse from my experience. I place these facts before you in all humility for the simple reason that you may know this land better, the land to which you have come to serve. You are here to find out the distress of the people of India and remove it. But I hope you are here also in a receptive mood, and if there is anything that India has to give, you will not stop your ears, you will not close your eyes, and steel your hearts, but open up your ears, eyes and most of all your hearts to receive all that may be good in this land. I give you my assurance that there is a great deal of good in India. Do not flatter yourselves with the belief that a mere recital of that celebrated verse in St. John makes a man a Christian. If I have read the Bible correctly, I know many men who have never heard the name of Jesus Christ or have even rejected the official interpretation of Christianity will, probably, if Jesus came in our midst today in the flesh, be owned by him more than many of us. I therefore ask you to approach the problem before you with open-heartedness and humility.

I was engaged in a friendly conversation with some missionaries this morning. I do not want to relate that conversation. But I do want to say that they are fine specimens of humanity. They did not want to misunderstand me, but I had to pass nearly one hour and a half in my attempt to explain to them that in writing what I had written I had not written anything in a spirit of ill-will or hatred towards Englishmen. I was hard put to it to carry that conviction. In fact I do not know whether I carried that conviction to them at all. If salt loseth its savour, wherewith shall it be salted? If I could not drive home the truth that was in me to the three friends who certainly came with open minds, how should I fare with others? It has often occurred to me that a seeker after truth has to be silent. I know the wonderful efficacy of silence. I visited a Trappist monastery in South Africa. A beautiful place it was. Most of the inmates of that place were under a vow of silence. I enquired of the Father the motive of it, and he said that the motive was apparent. 'We are frail human beings. We do not know very often what we say. If we want to listen to the still small voice that is always speaking within us, it will not be heard if we continually speak.' I understood that precious lesson. I know the secret of silence. I do not know just now as I speak to you whether it would not have been wise if I had said nothing to those friends beyond saying, 'We shall know each other better when the mists have rolled away.' As I speak to you, I feel humiliated. Why did I argue with these friends? But I say these things to you first of all to make this confession, and secondly to tell you also that, if you will refuse to see the other side, if you will refuse to understand what India is thinking, then you will deny yourselves the real privilege of service. I have told my missionary friends, 'Noble as you are, you have isolated yourselves from the people whom you want to serve.' I cannot help recalling to you the conversation I related in Darjeeling at the missionary Language School. Lord Salisbury was waited upon by a deputation of missionaries in connection with China and this deputation wanted protection. I cannot recall the exact words but give you the purport of the answer Lord Salisbury gave. He said, 'Gentlemen, if you want to go to China to preach the message of Christianity, then do not ask for assistance of the temporal power. Go with your lives in your hands and, if the people of China want to kill you, imagine that you have been killed in the service of God.' Lord Salisbury was right. Christian missionaries come to India under the shadow, or, if you like, under the protection of a temporal power, and it creates an impassable bar.

If you give me statistics that so many orphans have been reclaimed and brought to the Christian faith, I would accept them but I do not feel convinced thereby that it is your mission. In my opinion your mission is infinitely superior to that. You want to find men in India and, if you want to do that, you will have to go to the lowly cottages not to give them something, might be to take something from them. A true friend as I claim to be of the missionaries of India and of the Europeans, I speak to you what I feel from the bottom of my heart. I miss receptiveness, humility, willingness on your part to identify yourselves with the masses of India. I have talked straight from my heart. May it find a response from your hearts.

At the end of the address questions were invited. The

most important questions and their answers are given below:

*Q.* How do you think should the missionaries identify themselves with the masses?

*A.* The question is somewhat embarrassing. But I would venture to say, 'Copy Charlie Andrews.'

*Q.* What definite work would you suggest that a missionary should do for and among the masses?

*A.* Since I have been challenged I must unhesitatingly answer. 'The spinning wheel'. You naturally laugh, but if you knew the masses as I do, you will look upon this very simple instrument of torture (*takli*) with seriousness. You cannot present the hungry and famished masses with God. Their God is their food. General Booth knew what he was doing when at his numerous depots the first thing he did to the hungry men and women who flocked there was to give them a plate of soup. Before he would give them their next meal he called upon them to make splinters for his match factory and then he introduced them to God. The famished millions are famishing not because there is not enough food produced in India but because they have no work to do. The only work for the millions is the spinning wheel. I know the Industrial Mission House in Calcutta. It is good in its way, but it does not touch even the fringe of the question. The problem is how to take work to the cottages of these men, cottages which are scattered over a surface 1900 miles long and 1500 broad. They will not take the spinning wheel unless they learn the art themselves and unless they spin to set an example to these men who have lost faith in themselves and faith in everything and everybody. And the spinning wheel is useless unless you and I wear Khadi. Hence it is that I have not hesitated to say to Lord Reading or to Lord Willingdon that I will not be satisfied unless they and their orderlies are dressed from top to toe in Khadi.

*Q.* Do you definitely feel the presence of the living Christ within you?

*A*. If it is the historical Jesus surnamed Christ that you refer to, I must say I do not. If it is an adjective signifying one of the names of God, then I must say I do feel the presence of God—call Him Christ, call Him Krishna, call Him Rama. We have one thousand names to denote God, and if I did not feel the presence of God within me, I see so much of misery and disappointment every day that I would be a raving maniac and my destination would be the Hooghli.

*Young India*, 6-8-'25

12

## FOR CHRISTIAN FRIENDS

"Dear Br. Gandhi,

Under a double prompting when praying for you, I sit down to write. You have had your name blazoned abroad all over the (so-called) civilized world, as one of the greatest philosophers and sacrificial workers on earth. In India you have been proclaimed *the* Mahatma, and actually worshipped as one of *the* incarnations of India's many deities, and much as you have declared that you do not encourage these ascriptions of sanctity, you would indeed be more than human if you did not occasionally feel a sweet complacency in them. Your practice also of fasting when sin has been committed, or quarrels have taken place in your Ashram or schools has had a tendency to make Indians believe that you can merit blessing which can be communicated to others,—but has anybody been loving and courageous enough to write and challenge you as to how personally you are going to obtain atonement for your own sin? All your self-denials and fastings and prayer and good deeds cannot blot out one sin of your early days. For thirty or more years of your life you lived the carnal self life, seeking and following your own plans and ambitions without seeking to know God's purpose for your life or to honour His holy name. You were a trustee of talents intended to be used for the glory of God and the good of your fellowmen. Nothing that you do can obliterate the record of those years of indifference and disobedience. Every hour of every day of that period at least lifts up its voice in condemnation. Law must be vindicated. Some punishment must be inflicted. But even on earth it is a recognized principle that the prerogative of an earthly king is to have mercy—and yet righteousness must be the very foundation from which mercy may flow. The Laws of the Universe proclaim the impartial justice of the Creator and confirm the Bible declaration: 'The soul that sinneth, it shall die,' and yet the doctrine of vicarious suffering is written in the very nature of human existence. God is love. Every pulse of love in every creature has its origin and activity from Him. Parental, mother love, all love is a manifestation of or emanation from the fountain of the Divine Love. Milton sings:

'Oft ere the kindred source be down
The kindred blood will claim his own
And throbbing pulses silently
Move heart to heart in sympathy.'

'If all sin is sin against God,' (Psalm 51) the prerogative of forgiveness is His. If His righteous judgment is appeased by (For God was in Christ, reconciling the world unto Himself, not imputing their trespasses unto them) Himself suffering the death penalty on behalf of the race; and if, as in Phillipeans (II. 6-11) He commends everyone in heaven and on earth to accept Christ as Saviour and Lord to *the glory of God the Father*—how shall we (how will you) escape if you neglect so great a salvation?

Even if, as you profess to believe, Christ was only one of many incarnations of God, and the latest of them, you must either accept His tremendous claims as of Divine origin, or reject them as only human and fallible. And when He declares as He did to the Jews of His day—'If ye believe not that I am He, ye shall die in your sins,' or 'I am *the* way, *the* truth, and *the* life, no man cometh unto the Father, but by me,' you must either believe Him to have been self-deceived, or deliberately false. I see no other solution. I pray daily that Christ may grant you a revelation of Himself as He did to Saul of Tarsus, that before you pass off this earthly scene, you may be used to proclaim to India's millions the sacrificial efficacy of His precious blood.

Yours lovingly in His glad service."

This is a typical letter from an old English friend who regularly writes such letters almost every six months. This friend is very earnest and well known to me. But there are numerous other correspondents unknown to me who write in the same strain without arguing. Since now I cannot for reasons of health write to individual writers, I use this letter as a text for a general reply. Incidentally this effort will enable the readers of *Harijan*, who accept my guidance, to understand the nature of my religious belief.

My correspondent is a literalist. He gives its literal meaning to every text of the Bible in spite of its clear statement that "the letter killeth, the spirit giveth life." My very first reading of the Bible showed me that I would be repelled by many things in it if I gave their literal meaning to many texts or even took every passage in it as the word of God. I found, as I proceeded with my study of the scriptures of the various religions, that every scripture had to be treated likewise, not excepting the Vedas or the Upanishads. Therefore the story of the immaculate conception when I interpret it mystically does not repel me. I should find it hard to believe in the literal meaning of the verses relating to the immaculate conception of Jesus. Nor would it deepen my regard for Jesus if I gave those verses their literal meaning. This does not mean that the writers of the Gospels were untruthful persons. They wrote in a mood of exaltation. From my youth upward I learnt the art of estimating the value of scriptures on the basis of their ethical teaching. Miracles, therefore, had no interest for me. The miracle said to have been performed by Jesus, even if I had believed them literally, would not have reconciled me to any teaching that did not satisfy universal ethics. Somehow or other, words of religious teachers have for me, as I presume for millions, a living force which the same words uttered by ordinary mortals do not possess.

Jesus then to me is a great world teacher among others. He was to the devotees of his generation no doubt 'the only begotten son of God'. Their belief need not be mine. He affects my life no less because I regard him as one among the many begotten sons of God. The adjective 'begotten' has, for me, a deeper and possibly a grander meaning than its literal meaning. For me it implies spiritual birth. In his own times he was the nearest to God.

Jesus atoned for the sins of those who accepted his teachings by being an infallible example to them. But the example was worth nothing to those who never troubled to change their lives. A regenerate outgrows the original taint even as purified gold outgrows the original alloy.

I have made the frankest admission of my many sins. But I do not carry their burden on my shoulders. If I am journeying Godward, as I feel I am, it is safe with me. For I feel the warmth of the sunshine of His presence. My austerities, fastings and prayers are, I know, of no value, if I rely upon them for reforming me. But they have an inestimable value, if they represent, as I hope they do, the yearnings of a soul striving to lay his weary head in the lap of his Maker.

The Gita has become for me the key to the scriptures of the world. It unravels for me the deepest mysteries to be found in them. I regard them with the same reverence that I pay to the Hindu scriptures. Hindus, Mussalmans, Christians, Parsis, Jews are convenient labels. But when I tear them down, I do not know which is which. We are all children of the same God. "Verily verily I say unto you, not every one that sayeth unto me Lord, Lord, shall enter the Kingdom of heaven, but he that doeth the will of my Father which is in heaven shall enter the Kingdom," was said, though in different words, by all the great teachers of the world.

*Harijan*, 18-4-'36

## 13

# AS OTHERS SEE US

Here is a letter which has been lying on my file for some time:

"Your attitude towards religious conversion and particularly the hope you entertain for the Depressed Classes within the fold of Hinduism, overlooks the prevalent practices of Hinduism as it exists in India today. It is impossible not to acknowledge the beauty and the sublimity of Hinduism expounded by Vivekanand and Sir S. Radhakrishnan. But is that the Hinduism that is taught to the masses of India or practised by the heads of Hindu religion? What are the millions of the poor Indian people—starving millions as you call them—living in seven lakhs of villages seeking? Their first need is proper food, shelter and clothing so that they may be raised above the level of animals. Are the Depressed Classes anxious for temple entry?

Any religion is judged by its fruits. Here is a contrast. Take the case of the Christian religion, whether Roman Catholic or Protestant. The funds that are collected from the rich and poor are carefully accounted for and repaid in the form of medical and educational service. Religious worship is open to all alike. The number of schools, colleges, dispensaries, hospitals and orphanages admirably served by their religious institution bear eloquent testimony to the quality of faith that is in them. It is not a theology and philosophy which they possess but the self-sacrificing service which they render in abundant measure towards all that is a contrast to the service rendered by the temples and mutts. What are the uses of the wealth of temples and mutts? Are not these weapons of superstition and oppression? The heads of these mutts live princely lives with vast endowments, and when they care to stir out there is a huge retinue of palanquins, cars, elephants, camels and a host of disciples, descending on unhappy villages and towns, like locusts, for further collections. Their disciples who are priests are spread like spies throughout the districts, to collect money from the followers of various faiths, Madhvas, Lingayats, Shaivaites and so forth, under pain of excommunication or ostracism. I am informed that there are regular lawyers to collect dues and serve the interests of these religious heads, swamis and gurus. This state of affairs is an oppression worse than popery in its worst days. Not merely the accumulated wealth and the annual collections, which in all these mutts must amount to several crores, are never properly accounted for, but this gigantic system of ghastly exploitation continues to be supported by the most intellectual leaders of the people as if Hindu Society will break up by questioning it. This is practical Hinduism. Why should there be any surprise that the Depressed Classes alone should revolt against a system which denies equal rights to worship the Deity but keeps them also in perpetual social excommunication? Why is it that no one ventures to question the priestly oppression, this draining away annually the wealth of the people without any service whatever? While the millions are hungry, ignorant and illiterate, even a small proportion of wealth of the mutts and the temples is not turned to relieve human misery. Hinduism is so spiritual that it will not do it. Are the Hindu gods so ravenous that they require such an annual collection with complete indifference to those who give it? I doubt!

While the produce of the land is steadily drained away as land revenue on the one side by the State and religious extortion on the other, is it any wonder millions are underfed and poverty-stricken? Is it any relief to them to be told to work harder and more systematically in their leisure months after the harvest? What is taken in money and kind should return to them in the form of service they most need. If the poor unfortunate masses of India are not supported by the wealth of the Hindu mutts to shake off their illiteracy, ignorance, hook-worm, malaria, leprosy, diarrhoea, dysentery, cholera and plague—physical ills which they cannot at present get over without relief—they will never be capable of bringing greater intelligence to bear upon the resources of Nature. It is exploitation by religious heads that has crushed the people, and the money-lender and the State combined have finished the process. It is not more work and harder work, and the variety of cottage industries that these half dead half living masses require, but more vocational schools and dispensaries, maternity and child welfare centres and better food. They have paid for it in full and have been cheated out of the services they ought to get from religion and the State. When will the children of the villages have the light of morning in their eyes? In the process of evolution, to think that all that is dross in Hinduism will drop off like surface excrescence is as much as hoping that all that is vile in the present Government will also do the same by just wishing for it. If the State is not moved very easily by your herculean endeavours, Hinduism requires a far more drastic purge as it has been established some thousands of years longer than this alien Government. I would rather love the State that renders services of all sorts for the revenue collected than this religion which does nothing.

Bishops and priests of the Christian religion, in spite of the fierce criticism levelled against them in this land and every other country, render humanitarian service unequalled by any other class of human beings who follow any other faith or no faith, and are approachable to all people. Christian missions, far from being wealthy, have become poorer and lost all their Western supporters who today acknowledge the greatness of Hinduism and challenge them to go forth and serve their fellowmen with their own money. If the humanitarian service of the Christian heads are acknowledged, it is far better to give to them some of the resources that are now misused so that with their honest and excellent organization they may expand their humane service which the masses sorely need. What has Hinduism done for the villages, the most depressing morbid places under the sun? Nothing! Absolutely nothing! Government officials require *batta* to visit these places, and no wonder. One would welcome cheerfully the mechanical civilization of the West, but even that under Hindu hands becomes as vile as Bombay chawls. Anyone with open unprejudiced eyes can see it. You have no objection to accept missionary humanitarian service and yet will not consider what form of service Hinduism renders with its accumulated wealth in temples and mutts. When these religious institutions serve the poor regardless of caste, creed or community, instead of exploiting their abysmal superstition, Hinduism will really begin to live."

It is good to see ourselves as others see us. Try as we may, we are never able to know ourselves fully as we are, especially the evil side of us. This we can do only if we are not angry with our critics but will take in good part whatever they might have to say. Anyway I propose to examine the foregoing criticism as dispassionately as I can. The grave limitations of Hinduism as it is seen today in practice must be admitted. Many mutts and their administration are undoubtedly a disgrace to Hinduism. The money that is poured into some of them does not return to the worshippers in the form of service. This state of things must be ended or mended.

Humanitarian work done by Christian missions must also be admitted.

But these admissions of mine must not be interpreted to mean endorsement of the deductions of the writer. Economic and educational relief is required by most poor Indians in common with Harijans. But the latter suffer from special disabilities. It is not a question of what disabilities they resent. It is the duty of the so-called superior Hindus to break the chains that bind the Harijans even though they may hug them. The admission by the writer of the sublimity of Hinduism as expounded by Vivekanand and Radhakrishnan should have led to his discovery of its percolation down to the masses. I make bold to say that, in spite of the crudeness which one sees among the villagers, class considered, in all that is good in human nature they compare favourably with any villagers in the world. This testimony is borne out by the majority of travellers who from the times of Huen Tsang down to the present times have recorded their impressions. The innate culture that the villages of India show, the art which one sees in the homes of the poor, the restraint with which the villagers conduct themselves, are surely due to the religion that has bound them together from time immemorial.

In his zeal to belittle Hinduism, the writer ignores the

broad fact that Hinduism has produced a race of reformers who have successfully combated prejudices, superstitions and abuses. Without any drum-beating Hinduism has devised a system of relief of the poor which has been the envy of many foreign admirers. I myself feel that it leaves much to be desired. It has its evil side. But from the philanthropic standpoint it has wholly justified itself. It is not the Indian habit to advertise charities through printed reports and the like. But he who runs may see the free kitchens and free medical relief given along indigenous lines.

The writer belittles village work. It betrays gross ignorance. If the mutts and the revenue offices were extinguished and free schools were opened, the people would not be cured of their inertia. Mutts must be reformed, the revenue system must be overhauled, free primary schools must be established in every village. But starvation will not disappear because people pay no revenue and mutts are destroyed and schools spring up in every village. The greatest education in the villages consists in the villagers being taught or induced to work methodically and profitably all the year round whether it be on the land or at industries connected with the villages.

Lastly, my correspondent seems to resent acceptance by us of humanitarian services by missionaries. Will he have an agitation led against these missionary institutions? Why should they have non-Christian aid? They are established with the view of weaning Indians from their ancestral faith even as expounded by Vivekanand and Radhakrishnan. Let them isolate the institutions from the double purpose. It will be time enough then to expect non-Christian aid. The critic must be aware of the fact that even as it is some of these institutions do get non-Christian aid. My point is that there should be no complaint if they do not receive such aid so long as they have an aim which is repugnant to the non-Christian sentiment.

*Harijan*, 6-3-'37

## 14

## HOW CAN OTHERS HELP?

[From a speech delivered by Gandhiji before a Christian audience at the Leonard Theological College, Jubbulpore on 7th December 1933.]

Having made these introductory remarks, it is easy for me now to tell you on what terms you can give your assistance to the anti-untouchability movement. You should work in co-operation with, and if I may say it, in subordination to, the Society that has been formed for suppression and eradication of untouchability, namely, the Servants of Untouchables Society. That is to say, you should put your talents at the disposal of the Society. I do not mean metallic talents. These have to come from those who have to make repentance and reparation. I have seen during the few days of my tour that millions are ready for the reform. They can tangibly signify their support only by giving their coppers. But men and women of intelligence are wanted to work for the Harijans in a variety of ways. For the so-called Caste Hindus to serve the Harijans in a constructive manner is to get off their backs, to go down on their knees to them, to treat Harijan children as their own and Harijan men and women as blood brothers and sisters. It is almost a superhuman task and cannot be done without Divine aid. But Divine aid comes largely through human agency. I confess that we have too few teachers and other professional men and women in our ranks. We want to cope with the ever-increasing demand. I invite the aid of agencies like yours in this work. You will now understand what I mean by subordination. This is the right way.

But there is also the wrong way. You may choose to work independently. You may have the conversion of Harijans to Christianity. You may see in the movement a chance for propaganda. If you work among the Harijans with such an aim, you can see that the very end we have in view will be frustrated. If you believe that Hinduism is a gift, not of God but of Satan, quite clearly you cannot accept my terms. You and I would be dishonest if we did not make clear to one another what we stand for.

*Harijan*, 15-12-'33

## 15

## ABOUT 'CONVERSION'

Mr. A. A. Paul of the Federation of International Fellowships asked me the other day to define in these columns my position on 'conversion'. I told him to frame definite questions on which he would like my answers. The result was the following letter with a list of propositions attached:

> "You remember that a little over a month ago, I wrote to you asking you whether you would publish a statement giving your views on 'conversion'. You wrote back to say that it would be easier for you if we could put them in the form of questions or assertions. At the request of the Executive Committee of the Madras International Fellowship, one of our Christian members has prepared the enclosed statement, and the Committee has asked me to pass it on to you with the request that you will kindly find it possible to answer these statements in *Harijan*. Of course you will notice that the questions are framed from the Christian point of view; but the Committee feels that the questions will apply equally well to other Missionary Religions which are engaged in conversion programme. May I hope that you will find it possible to explain your attitude to these questions?
>
> 1. Conversion is a change of heart from sin to God. It is the work of God. Sin is separation from God.
>
> 2. The Christian believes that Jesus is the fulfilment of God's revelation to mankind, that He is our Saviour from sin, that He alone can bring the sinner to God and thus enable him to live.

3. The Christian, to whom God has become a living reality and power through Christ, regards it as his privilege and duty to speak about Jesus and to proclaim the free offer which He came on earth to make.

4. If any man's heart is so moved by the hearing of this message as to repent and wish to live a new life as a disciple of Jesus, the Christian regards it as right to admit him to the Company of His professed believers which is called the Christian Church.

5. The Christian shall do all in his power to sound the sincerity of conviction in all such cases and shall point out, as he can, the consequences of such a step, stressing the duty a man owes to his family.

6. The Christian shall do everything in his power to prevent any motives of self-seeking on his part and of material considerations on the part of the convert.

7. Inasmuch as Jesus came to give full life, and that as a matter of history conversion has often meant an enhancing of personality, the Christian shall not be accused of using material inducements if conversion results in the social uplift of the convert—it always being understood that such shall never be used as a means to an end.

8. The Christian is right in accepting as his duty the care of the sincere convert, body, soul and mind.

9. It shall not be brought against the Christian that he is using material inducements, when certain facts in Hindu social theory, out of his control, are in themselves an inducement to the Harijan. (But see points 5 and 6.)"

In order to understand the background to these propositions, the reader should know that the origin of the main question was a discussion I was carrying on with Mr. A. A. Paul on the so-called mass conversion of a village predominantly or wholly composed of Harijans. The reader may later on read more of this 'conversion'. For the present purpose it is enough that he understands that it is the method of mass conversion that has to be tested in the light of these propositions. Indeed the ninth proposition almost says as much.

I have read the propositions several times, and the more I read them the more I feel that they can be applied only to individual contacts, never to the mass of mankind. Take the very first proposition. Sin is defined to be 'separation from God'. 'Conversion is a change of heart from sin to God. It is the work of God.' So says the author of the propositions. If conversion is the work of God, why should that work be taken away from Him? And who is man to take away anything from God? He may become a humble instrument in the hands of God. Even so he cannot be judge of men's hearts. I often wonder whether we are always true judges of our own hearts. 'Man, know thyself' must have been wrung out of a desperate heart. And if we know so little of ourselves, how much less must we know of our neighbours and remote strangers who may differ from us in a multitude of things, some of which are of the highest moment! The second proposition deals with the Christian belief handed to the believer from generation to generation, the truth of which thousands of Christians born are never called upon to test for themselves, and rightly not. Surely it is a dangerous thing to present it to those who have been brought up to a different belief. And it would appear to me to be impertinent on my part to present my untested belief to the professor of another which for aught I know may be as true as mine. It is highly likely that mine may be good enough for me and his for him. A thick woollen coat would be the thing for one living in the cold regions of the earth, as a piece of loin-cloth for another living near the equatorial regions.

The third proposition too, like the first, relates to the mysteries of religion which are not understood by the common people who take them in faith. They work well enough among people living in the traditional faith. They will repel those who have been brought up to believe something else.

The other five propositions deal with the conduct of the missionary among those whom he is seeking to convert. They seem to me to be almost impossible of application in practice. The start being wrong, all that follows must be necessarily so. Thus how is the Christian to sound the sincerity of the conviction of his hearers? By a temporary trial? Any test that can be conceived will fail even to be reasonably conclusive. No one but God knows a man's heart. Is the Christian so sure of his being so right in body, mind and soul as to feel comfortably "right in accepting as his duty the care of the sincere convert, body, soul and mind"?

The last proposition—the crown of all the preceding ones—takes one's breath away. For it makes it clear that the other eight are to be applied in all their fulness to the poor Harijans. And yet the very first proposition has not ceased to puzzle the brains of some of the most intellectual and philosophical persons even in the present generation. Who knows the nature of original sin? What is the meaning of separation from God? What is that of the union with God? What are the signs of him who is united to God? Are all who dare to preach the message of Jesus the Christ sure of their union with God? If they are not, who will test the Harijans' knowledge of these deep things?

This is my reaction to the foregoing propositions. I hope no Christian who reads it will be offended by it. I would have been false to my numerous Christian friends, if I had hidden from them my true position on the nine propositions.

My own detached view may now be stated in a few words. I believe that there is no such thing as conversion from one faith to another in the accepted sense of the term. It is a highly personal matter for the individual and his God. I may not have any design upon my neighbour as to his faith which I must honour even as I honour my own. For I regard all the great religions of the world as true at any rate for the people professing them as mine is true for me. Having reverently studied the scriptures of the world, I have no difficulty in perceiving the beauties in all of them. I could no more think of asking a Christian or a

Mussalman or a Parsi or a Jew to change his faith than I would think of changing my own. This makes me no more oblivious of the limitations of the professors of those faiths, than it makes me of the grave limitations of the professors of mine. And seeing that it takes all my resources in trying to bring my practice to the level of my faith and in preaching the same to my co-religionists, I do not dream of preaching to the followers of other faiths. 'Judge not lest ye be judged', is a sound maxim for one's conduct. It is a conviction daily growing upon me that the great and rich Christian missions will render true service to India, if they can persuade themselves to confine their activities to humanitarian service without the ulterior motive of converting India or at least her unsophisticated villagers to Christianity, and destroying their social superstructure, which, notwithstanding its many defects, has stood now from time immemorial the onslaughts upon it from within and from without. Whether they—the missionaries—and we wish it or not, what is true in the Hindu faith will abide, what is untrue will fall to pieces. Every living faith must have within itself the power of rejuvenation if it is to live.

*Harijan*, 28-9-'35

## 16

## ADI KARNATAKAS

All the readers of *Young India* may not know who Adi Karnatakas are. They are the suppressed classes of Karnatak. Just as at the Raniparaj Conference, friends of the Raniparaj altered the name Kaliparaj to the more appropriate name Raniparaj, so the suppressed classes all over India have been not unnaturally taking for themselves names which have no bad odour about them. In this spirit the suppressed classes in Karnatak describe themselves as Adi Karnatakas. And so I notice under that heading two paragraphs in the address of the Diwan of Mysore to its Representative Assembly. One observes from these paragraphs that 'exceptional facilities have been created for the education of the members of these classes, and methods have been adopted to suit their special circumstances.' 'Among these methods are scholarships, exemptions from school fees, a free supply of clothes and school requisites, free hostels; and over and above the right of admission to all schools, 605 special schools have been provided for them. There are altogether 16,575 students of this class receiving tuition in Mysore.' 'An attempt is being made to organize a co-operative agricultural scheme with due provision of land, livestock and direction.'

The paragraphs end with the following suggestion:

> "These people ought to be the strength of our strength. Shall we let them become our weakness? They have a rankling sense of wrong which only kindness can heal. The aim should be to 'Hinduize' them more and more, for they belong to the Hindu community, and to offer them every facility to remain within the fold. They will be a mighty accession to the strength of our body politic; if not, they will be an equally heavy subtraction from it. Alienated, they will introduce an additional element of heterogeneity which will further complicate the already difficult problems of administration. No possible means of amelioration should be neglected, and every friend of Hindu society, every lover of Mysore, should supplement the efforts of Government with all his strength."

This suggestion is a gentle warning both to the Christian missionary and the Mussalman missionary not to try to wean these suppressed classes from Hinduism but, if they at all wish to interfere, to act so that they may become better Hindus. If the suggestion is acted upon by the parties concerned, it will be a substantial contribution towards the attainment of real peace in the land.

*Young India*, 7-7-'27

17

## DO NOT ENTICE HARIJANS

If the leaders of different religions in India ceased to compete with one another for enticing Harijans into their fold, it would be well for this unfortunate country. I have the profound conviction that those who are engaged in the competition are not serving the cause of Religion. By looking at it in terms of politics or economics they reduce the religious values, whereas the proper thing would be to estimate politics and every other thing in terms of religion. Religion deals with the science of the soul. Great as the other forces of the world are, if there is such a thing as God, soul force is the greatest of all. We know as a matter of fact that the greater the force the finer it is. Hitherto electricity has held the field among the finer physical powers. And yet nobody has seen it except through its wonderful results. Scientific speculation dares to talk of a force finer even than that of electricity. But no instrument devised by man has been able to know anything positive of soul force or spiritual force. It is on that force that the true religious reformer has hitherto relied and never without hope fulfilled. It is that force which will finally govern the welfare of Harijans and everyone else and confound the calculations of men however gifted they may be intellectually. The reformer who has entered upon the duty of ridding Hinduism of the disease of untouchability has to depend in everything he does on that force and nothing else.

*Harijan*, 22-8-'36

## 18

## WHAT IS A MIRACLE?

About the 9th of October last there was a meeting of Christian denominations in London. His Grace the Archbishop of Canterbury presided. The following occurs in the report of the meeting published in *The Church Times* of 16th October:

> "The next speaker was dressed as a layman, without even the smallest discernible purple patch to indicate that he was Dr. J. W. Pickett, a Bishop of the Methodist Episcopal Church, U. S. A. For some years past, Dr. Pickett has been studying the mass movements on the spot in India, and has published the results of his observations in *Christian Mass Movements in India,* described by the Archbishop of Canterbury as a remarkable and valuable book. Dr. Pickett is profoundly impressed with the spiritual significance of the movement. He said that four and a half millions of the depressed classes in India have become the disciples of our Lord, and the witness they bear to Him in their lives is making the multitudes in India marvel. Even Brahmins have testified—albeit reluctantly—to the power of Christianity to transform the characters and lives of people whom they once thought incapable of religious feelings, and to whom they denied the right of entrance to the temples of Hinduism. It is people of this kind, said Dr. Pickett, who have now standards of church attendance and worship difficult to equal in Western Christendom. He quoted an example in the Telugu area, where 900,000 people now profess the Christian Faith. Out of 1,026 villages, 1,002 hold a service for the worship of God every evening of the year, and more than two hundred also a daily morning service. It appealed to satisfy Dr. Pickett entirely as a test of the reality of the faith of the converts to hear a surprisingly high proportion of them speak of a sense of mystical union with God, and their belief that God had come into their lives. Even their Hindu neighbours admitted that the religion of Jesus Christ had lifted them to a

new standard of cleanliness of person and home, and made them a trustworthy people. More impressive still is the fact that high caste people are now coming into the Church, literally by dozens and hundreds, in areas where this transformation of life has occurred among the untouchables. 'It is a miracle,' he declared, 'one of the great miracles of Christian history.' "

I have rarely seen so much exaggeration in so little space. A reader ignorant of conditions in India would conclude that the figures relate to the conversions due to the movement led by Dr. Ambedkar. I am sure Dr. Pickett could not have made any such claim. He has in mind the figures to date commencing from the establishment of the first church in India hundreds of years ago. But the figures are irrelevant to the general claim said to have been advanced by the Bishop. Where are "the multitudes in India who marvel" at the transformation in the lives of "four and a half millions of the depressed classes"? I am one of the multitude having practically travelled more than half a dozen times all over India, and have not seen any transformation on the scale described by Dr. Pickett, and certainly none of recent date. I have had the privilege of addressing meetings of Indian Christians who have appeared to me to be no better than their fellows. Indeed the taint of untouchability persists in spite of the nominal change of faith so far as the social status is concerned. Needless to say I am referring to the masses, not individuals. I should like to know the Brahmins "who have testified—albeit reluctantly—to the power of Christianity to transform the characters and lives of people whom they once thought incapable of religious feeling". But if it is of any consequence, I can show many Brahmins who can testify to the power of the reform movement to make a radical change in the lives and outlook of Harijans who were neglected by Caste Hindus. I must pass by the other unbelievable generalizations. But I should like to know the hundreds of High Caste Hindus who "are now coming into the Church in areas where this transformation of life has occurred among the untouchables". If all the astounding statements Dr. Pickett has propounded can be substantiated, truly it is "one of the great miracles of Christian history", nay, of the history of man.

But do miracles need an oratorical demonstration? Should we in India miss such a grand miracle? Should we remain untouched by it? Miracles are their own demonstration. As witness the miracle in Travancore. Nobody believed a month ago that the more than 2,000 temples of Travancore could be opened to Harijans, and that Harijans would enter them in their hundreds without let or hindrance from the most orthodox Hindus. Yet that event has happened in Travancore which even he who runs may see. It is beside the point whether it can be called a miracle or not. I see in it the visible finger of the Invisible God.

I believe in the Bible as I believe in the Gita. I regard all the great faiths of the world as equally true with my own. It hurts me to see any one of them caricatured as they are today by their own followers and as has been done by the learned Bishop, assuming of course that the report reproduced above is substantially correct.

***Harijan*, 19-12-'36**

## 19

## CHURCH MISSIONARY SOCIETY

The Church Missionary Society of England has published a pamphlet prepared by Prebendary W. W. Cash, in which

> "The C. M. S. is appealing for an emergency fund of £ 25,000 to enable extra grants to be made during the next five years to those areas where this big movement is taking place, and the Society appeals to the whole Church to support it in this effort. Not for ourselves do we ask people to give, but for the sake of the hundreds of thousands who are dimly groping after Christ, and who are finding spiritual life and social uplift through the Gospel."

'The big movement' referred to is the movement for the conversion of Harijans. The money is wanted for work in the Telugu area and Travancore.

The appeal ends thus:

> "The movement among the outcastes is spreading to the caste-people, and within the last five years it is estimated that no less than 30,000 caste-people from fifty-one different castes have become Christians. This is a movement of such far-reaching consequences that we dare not refuse help. The thousands of today may become millions tomorrow. Will you help us to go forward in a great advance that the harvest may be reaped?"

Its opening sentences run as follows:

> "Recent news in the papers has attracted widespread attention to the untouchables of India. We have read of great conferences of outcaste peoples who have decided to break away from Hinduism. We have heard of mass movements towards Christianity, and of baptisms of tens of thousands of converts in recent years. We have followed with growing interest the development of the young churches in these rural areas, particularly in the Dornakal and Travancore Dioceses. We are therefore compelled to examine more closely what is happening in India and to see how far we are reaping the harvest which has come."

It contains among others these three headlines:

1. "What is happening among these people?"
2. "Who is Dr. Ambedkar?"
3. "What does India say to Dr. Ambedkar's advice?"

I cull the following from what appears under the third headline:

> "There is no doubt that there have been important repercussions all over India from the conference of untouchables. Mr. Gandhi had previously carried on a campaign for the removal of untouchability, but he has signally failed because he clung to the Hindu system which has been the cause of the trouble."

In passing I may remark that I am utterly unconscious of "signal failure". I have not clung to "the Hindu system which has been the cause of the trouble". On the contrary I have rejected that which has been the cause of the trouble, namely untouchability. And I have not abandoned the campaign as suggested in the quotation.

Under the same headline occurs also this paragraph:

> "In the C. M. S. area of the Dornakal Diocese there are no less than three hundred villages appealing for teachers; they represent forty thousand people definitely asking for baptism. The Bishop reckons that probably about a million people in his diocese are moving Christward."

Though I have travelled in the Telugu area often enough I have never heard of forty thousand Harijans asking for baptism or any figure near it.

Under the same headline occurs also this precious paragraph:

> "In Travancore, the Ezhava community are definitely on trek. They are a superior type of the 'exterior' castes. Many of them are educated; some are landowners, others lawyers, doctors, officials and teachers; but they are excluded from the temples and suffer from the disabilities of the outcaste community. The leaders of one section of these people numbering over 850,000 have waited on the Bishop in Travancore, because they are anxious that their entire community should become Christians. This is by no means entirely due to Dr. Ambedkar, but is another incident in a situation which is growing in magnitude from day to day."

I dare not speak for the Ezhava leaders. The papers report them to have congratulated the Maharaja on his Proclamation. But that may not be inconsistent with their anxiety that their entire community should become Christians. Let them speak, if they will, on the contents of the quotation.

The exaggerations of Bishop Pickett, with which I had the misfortune of dealing last week, are beaten perhaps by those contained in the appeal.

There is no other way to deal with the exaggerations of which the appeal is full than by living them down and by the truth working through the lives of the reformers. The appeal deals not with the past but with contemporary events. And if millions are waiting to bear witness to the message of Christ, as and in the form in which it comes through the agents of the C. M. S., my disbelief in the statements made in the appeal will melt like snow under the rays of the mid-day sun.

*Harijan*, 26-12-'36

## 20

## THE COW AND THE HARIJAN

The cow is an object of worship and veneration to millions in India. I count myself among them. The cow-shed in Segaon is in front of me. I cannot escape its inmates even if I would. And when I was arguing the question of the masses of Harijans with Christian friends, I said, 'The majority of Harijans can no more understand the presentation of Christianity than my cows.' This comparison shocked my friends so much that the shock has travelled to America and I have begun to receive letters from America telling me how my comparison is being used to discredit me and my claim to serve Harijans. The critics seem to say, 'You can have little regard for Harijans, if you compare them to the cow.'

Nevertheless I am unrepentant. My American credit will be little worth if it can be demolished on the very first shock however trivial it might be. But I hold that my comparison was as innocuous as it was appropriate. It was innocuous because of the unique place the cow occupies in India. It was appropriate because in the matter of understanding the presentation of Christianity the ordinary Harijan can no more take it in than the cow. That the dullest

Harijan can be trained to understand it in course of time, whereas the cow never can, is irrelevant for the simple reason that the discussion related to the present condition, not to future possibility. My point would be better understood if I extend the comparison and say that my five year old grandson or my sixty-eight year old wife can no more understand the presentation than my cows, though both my wife and my grandson are objects of tender care and attention. I could say of myself that I can no more read the Chinese alphabet today than my worshipful cow. The truth of this last statement is not in any way altered by the fact that, if someone began to teach my cow and me the difficult alphabet, I should beat the cow hollow, if the poor venerable mother ever consented to enter the competition. Let my critics and credulous friends understand that, apart from the comparison, I stand on unassailable ground when I assert that it is a travesty of religion to seek to uproot from the Harijans' simple minds such faith as they have in their ancestral religion and to transfer their allegiance to another, even though that other may be as good as and equal to the original in quality. Though all soils have the same predominant characteristics, we know that the same seeds do not fare equally well in all soils. I have some excellent tree cotton seeds which thrive excellently in certain parts of Bengal. But Mirabehn has not succeeded as yet in getting the same result from the same seeds in the Varoda soil. But I should be unable to subscribe to the formula, if the attempt was made to advance it, that the Varoda soil is inferior to the Bengal soil. But my fear is that, though Christian friends nowadays do not say or admit that Hindu religion is untrue, they must harbour in their breasts the belief that Hinduism is an error and that Christianity as they believe it is the only true religion. Without some such thing it is not possible to understand, much less to appreciate, the C. M. S. appeal from which I reproduced in these columns some revealing extracts the other day. One could understand the attack on untouchability and many other errors that have crept into Hindu life. And if they would help us to get rid of the admitted abuses and purify our religion, they would do helpful constructive work which would be gratefully accepted. But so far as one can understand the present effort, it is to uproot Hinduism from the very foundation and replace it by another faith. It is like an attempt to destroy a house which though badly in want of repair appears to the dweller quite decent and habitable. No wonder he welcomes those who show him how to repair it and even offer to do so themselves. But he would most decidedly resist those who sought to destroy the house that had served well him and his ancestors for ages, unless he, the dweller, was convinced that the house was beyond repair and unfit for human habitation. If the Christian world entertains that opinion about the Hindu house, 'Parliament of Religions' and 'International Fellowship' are empty phrases. For both the terms presuppose equality of status, a common platform. There cannot be a common platform as between inferiors and superiors, or the enlightened and unenlightened, the regenerate and the unregenerate, the high-born and the low-born, the caste-man and the out-caste. My comparison may be defective, may even sound offensive. My reasoning may be unsound. But my proposition stands.

*Harijan*, 13-3-'37

## 21

## CONVERSION FOR CONVENIENCE

Presentation, with a view to conversion, of a faith other than one's own, can only necessarily be through an appeal to the intellect or the stomach or both. I do maintain that the vast mass of Harijans, and for that matter Indian humanity, cannot understand the presentation of Christianity, and that generally speaking their conversion wherever it has taken place has not been a spiritual act in any sense of the term. They are conversions for convenience. And I have had overwhelming corroboration of the truth during my frequent and extensive wanderings.

***Harijan*, 12-6-'37**

## 22

## SHAMEFUL IF TRUE

Thakkar Bapa sends me the following statement which he received during his recent tour in the Nizam's Dominions.

> "About six months ago an event which took place at Karepally, Warangal District, Nizam's Dominions, describes the methods adopted by the Christian missionaries to make conversions of Hindus and especially Harijans. Some days previous to the appointed date, the village teachers sent out news of the coming event into all the surrounding villages and made sure that the people of all Castes of Hindus and especially Harijans were present on the occasion in large numbers. Then the pastor arrived at the place bringing with him a girl, about 12 years old, who he said would cure all that were presented to her of all sorts of diseases and also show them the real path to realization of God.

The pastor then stood and said addressing those present, 'You believe in gods who are dead and gone. Your Rama was born, behaved and acted like an ordinary mortal and then died. So was the case with Krishna also, who had many more vices to his credit. Here is before you a person who is the very incarnation of Christ. Christ is in her now, which fact you can verify yourself by being cured of your diseases at the mere touch of her hands. Why believe in gods who are past and no more effective? You should all believe in and follow the path of Jesus Christ who was born to Virgin Mary, preached the Gospel which leads to salvation, died outwardly but rose again on the third day to redeem the sinning millions of the world.

A subscription of one anna per head and two annas for a metal cross were charged. They were told that, unless they wore the cross at all times and believed in the truth and efficacy of Christianity, there would not be any good effect in the case of diseased patients.

This happened on two occasions. On the third occasion, the Secretary of the District Committee and friends visited them and told them that they could preach their religion as they wanted to, but they should not wound the feelings of the people by repeating unpleasant things which were not true. The local police then stopped the proceedings fearing there might be breach of peace in the place."

If it is true, it stands self-condemned. I would like the Mission concerned to investigate the complaint and throw light on it.

*Harijan*, 5-6-'37

23

## HOW THEY CONVERT

Thakkar Bapa had his attention drawn to the so-called conversion to Christianity in Shahabad District (Bihar). He thereupon called for a report on the statements made to him. The following is the report made by the local Harijan Sevak Sangh:

> "In the district of Shahabad, about 40 years ago, a Methodist Episcopal Christian Mission was established at Arrah. Through its efforts a large number of Harijans, numbering about 3 thousand, were converted to Christianity up to the year 1931. These converts were drawn largely from the Rabidas (Chamar) community and are to be found mostly in thanas of Piro, Shahpur, Dumraon and Navanagar. Most of them embraced Christianity very soon after the Hindu-Muslim riots of 1917. This Mission has got a district officer with headquarters at Arrah and a number of subordinate officers and preachers—European and Indian, males and females—deputed to work in the interior. It has a very large establishment in about 60 acres of land at Arrah where it has got a number of permanent buildings in which they conduct boys' and girls' Middle English schools and an industrial and technical school. It has acquired residential lands and constructed buildings of its own, in all the sub-divisional towns and also in important villages in which weekly church gatherings take place regularly.
>
> Last year a Roman Catholic Mission appeared on the scene. Since then, the activities of both the Missions have increased. The Roman Catholic preachers first approached the former Christian (Protestant) converts and tried to take them within their fold. They have been successful in winning over many of them to their faith. They have now directed their efforts towards new conversions.
>
> The news that appeared in the papers last month purported to relate to the new conversions in Piro and Sahar thanas. On enquiry it has been found that practically there has been no conversion in Sahar thana. But the case

of Piro is different. It is the headquarters of the biggest and the most thickly populated thana of the district and the missionaries seem to have concentrated their efforts on it. Both of them have got their separate establishments here and have employed many preachers—male and female. The Roman Catholics have succeeded in bringing over many of the old Protestant converts of this thana to their denomination and are employing them to preach and propagate Christianity among the villagers. They have engaged the unemployed and literate old converts as teachers through whom their propaganda is carried on and new converts obtained. Enquiry has revealed that they have been successful in getting some new Christian converts from the Rabidas (Chamar) community amongst whom their activities are mainly confined. Roughly their method of work may be described as follows:

After having visited the village and created familiarity with the Harijans they at once start a school and put it in charge of a Harijan teacher who either himself is an influential man or related to such a one. Whenever they come to learn that some tension or actual litigation is going on between the Harijans and other villagers they at once seize the opportunity to take up the side of the poor Harijans and help them with money and advice. They are thus hailed as saviours and conversion follows as if to repay the obligation.

As their work is scattered throughout the thana in the remotest villages, the present enquiry could not be exhaustive. The exact number of villages affected and the total number of converts could not be accurately obtained. In thirteen villages in Thana Piro where the enquiry was held, the number of total converts would be about 600 out of whom about one-fourth are old and the rest new. Both the Missions are carrying on similar proselytizing activities in some other thanas with more or less success. A comprehensive enquiry for the collection of accurate and complete statistics seems to be urgently necessary. The one remarkable feature of these recent conversions is that they take place *en masse*. Whenever a village Harijan leader accepts the new faith almost all belonging to his clan follow him. Sometimes an influential Sardar is instrumental in converting people of his community living in several villages. It would thus appear that the propaganda is threatening to become highly contagious and the number may soon rise to something quite unexpected. In all cases of conversions new or old, not a single instance can be found in which the acceptance of the new faith was due to any religious conviction. The missionary propaganda bore fruit on account of the fact that the Harijans were extremely dissatisfied with their unbearable conditions and hoped to get rid of them by the change. The reasons, therefore, of conversions may be roughly described as economic or socio-economic. Generally, the Harijans have to submit to a number of unjust exactions and to suffer from humiliating treatment which are now resented by them. Resistance not unoften leads to quarrels which sometimes reach law courts. These conditions are exploited by the missionaries. But the conversions generally have no enduring character.

Most of the old converts are still following their old religious and social customs and ceremonies unchanged. Some of them have already reverted to their old faith. Those of the new and the old who are still continuing as nominal Christians are willing to return to Hinduism if their grievances are removed. Their grievances as disclosed during the enquiry are briefly indicated below:

1. They are forced to labour for their *maliks* and other Caste Hindus of their villages at about half or even less wages than they would get for the same kind of labour in other villages.

2. They are forced to labour for their *maliks* and other Caste Hindu villagers on occasions of marriages and deaths in their families on almost no wages.

3. They are charged 6 as. per year per family as mutharfa(house rent).

4. They have to pay Re. 1, Rs. 2 and Rs. 3 or 4 for the hide of every dead cow, bullock or buffalo respectively to their owners if they fail to deliver a corresponding number of pairs of shoes to them.

5. Their wives are paid only four annas for a male or two annas for a female child born in the house of the Caste Hindu villagers where they have to work as midwives during confinement, and even these payments are not regularly made.

6. They are forced to work for their *maliks* and Caste

Hindu villagers even at the sacrifice of their own agricultural needs or when they are ill or engaged in their social or religious functions.

7. The levy of the chowkidari tax on them is generally excessive.

8. They are not allowed to draw water from wells used by Caste Hindus.

9. They are not allowed to enter temples nor are Brahmin priests available to recite religious *kathas* at their houses."

If what is said in the report about the conversions be true, it is from my standpoint reprehensible. Such superficial conversions can only give rise to suspicion and strife. But if a missionary body or individuals choose to follow the methods described in the report, nothing can be done to prevent them. It is therefore much more profitable to turn the searchlight inward and to discover our own defects. Fortunately the report enables us to do so. Nine causes are enumerated to show why Harijans are induced to leave the Hindu fold. Seven are purely economic, one is social, and one is purely religious. Thus they are reduced economically, degraded socially, and boycotted from religious participation. The wonder is not that they leave Hinduism, the wonder is that they have not done so for so long and that so few leave their ancestral faith even when they do. The moral is obvious. Let us make every discovery such as the one made in Shahabad an occasion for greater self-purification, greater dedication to the Harijan cause, greater identification with the Harijans. It should result in the local Sangh collecting more workers than it has for doing on the one hand service among the Harijans and on the other propaganda among the so-called Caste Hindus, not in the shape of reviling them but showing them that religion does not warrant the treatment that is meted out to Harijans by them.

*Harijan*, 19-6-'37

## 24

## THE SOCIAL BAIT

A friend who has had occasion to study the work of the Salvation Army, sends me the following interesting note :

> "The Salvation Army is essentially a religious body with 'aggressive evangelism' as its main characteristic. The social work the Army does 'has from the first been regarded by the Army leaders as an organized warfare against social evils in order to clear the way of evangelization.' This is from the Encyclopaedia Britannica (14th edition). It further says that 'It was realized that the physical and the environmental condition of many of the people, especially in great cities, made it extremely difficult for them to apprehend the spiritual message which the Army had to deliver. Therefore various social activities arose, diverse in character but all actuated by the same purpose,' and General Booth himself in one of his letters to his son has said that 'The social work is the bait, but it is salvation that is the hook that lands the fish.'
>
> The object and the work of this Mission according to its Founder is 'to seek the conversion of the neglected crowds of people who are living without God and without hope, and to gather those so converted into Christian Fellowship.' It is also stated in the Salvation Army Year Book for 1937 that 'upon Salvationists everywhere was urged the importance of personal evangelism—that each one was responsible before God for the Salvation of others. Personal touch, personal conversation, personal effort, it was pointed out, was of paramount importance, nay, was the duty of every wearer of our uniform.' Thus 'Every Soldier a Soul-winner' became and remains an inspiring slogan."

Of course what is true of the Army is more or less true of all Christian Missions. Their social work is undertaken not for its own sake but as an aid to the salvation of those who receive social service. The history of India would have been written differently if the Christians had come to India to live their lives in our midst and permeate ours with their aroma if there was any. There would then have been mutual goodwill and utter absence of suspicion. But say some of them, 'If what you say had held good with Jesus, there would have been no Christians.' To answer this would land me in a controversy in which I have no desire to engage. But I may be permitted to say that Jesus preached not a new religion but a new life. He called men to repentance. It was he who said, 'Not every one that saith unto me, Lord, Lord, shall enter into the kingdom of heaven; but he that doeth the will of my Father which is in heaven.'

*Harijan*, 12-6-'37

25

## FOR CHRISTIAN INDIANS

[The other day I was privileged to address what was to be a meeting of Christian Indians predominantly. My address, therefore, took naturally a different shape from what it was to be. Nevertheless, I give below a brief summary of portions of the address, as, in my opinion, it is of interest to know what one, who has lived in their midst, amid various scenes and surroundings, has thought about and felt for them. —M. K. G.]

When I was a youth I remember a Hindu having become a convert to Christianity. The whole town understood that the initiation took the shape of this well-bred Hindu partaking of beef and brandy in the name of Jesus Christ and discarding his national costume. I learnt in later years that such a convert, as so many of my missionary friends put it, came to a life of freedom out of a life of bondage, to a life of plenty out of one of penury. As I wander about throughout the length and breadth of India I see many Christian Indians almost ashamed of their birth, certainly of their ancestral religion, and of their ancestral dress. The aping of Europeans on the part of Anglo-Indians is bad enough, but the aping of them by Indian converts is a violence done to their country and, shall I say, even to their new religion. There is a verse in the New Testament to bid Christians avoid meat if it would offend their neighbours. Meat here, I presume, includes drink and dress. I can appreciate uncompromising avoidance of all that is evil in the old, but where there is not only no question of any thing evil but where an ancient practice may be even desirable, it would be a crime to part with it when one knows for certain that the giving up would deeply hurt relatives and friends. Conversion must not mean denationalization. Conversion should mean a definite giving up of the evil of the old, adoption of all the good of the new and a scrupulous avoidance of everything evil in the new. Conversion, therefore, should mean a life of greater dedication to one's own country, greater surrender to God, greater self-purification. Years ago I met the late Kali Charan Banerjee. Had I not known before I went there that he was a Christian, I should certainly not have noticed from the outward appearance of his home that he was one. It was no different from an ordinary modern Hindu home,—simple and meagre in furniture. The great man was dressed like an ordinary un-Europeanized Hindu Bengali. I know that there is a marvellous change coming over Christian Indians. There is on the part of a large number of them a longing to revert to original simplicity, a longing to belong to the nation and to serve it, but the process is too slow. There need be no waiting. It requires not much effort, but I was told, and even as I write, I have a letter from a Christian Indian before me telling me that he and his friends find it difficult to make the change, because of the opposition of their superiors. Some of them tell me that they are even jealously watched, and any movement on their part to identify themselves with national movements is strongly condemned. The late Principal Rudra and I used often to discuss this evil tendency. I well remember how he used to deplore it. I am offering a tribute to the memory of a dead friend when I inform the reader that he used often to express his grief that it was too late in life for him to change some of the unnecessary European habits to which he was brought up. Is it not truly deplorable that many Christian Indians discard their own mother-tongue, bring up their children only to speak in English ? Do they not thereby completely cut themselves adrift from the nation in whose midst they have to live? But they may answer in self-defence that many Hindus and even Mussalmans have become denationalized. The *Tu Quoque* argument serves no useful purpose. I am writing not as a critic but as a friend who has enjoyed for the past thirty years the closest intimacy with hundreds of Christian Indians. I want my missionary friends and Christian Indians to reciprocate the spirit in which these lines are written. I write in the name and for the sake of heart unity which I want to see established among the people of this land professing different faiths. In nature there is a fundamental unity running through all the diversity we see about us. Religions are no exception to the natural law. They are given to mankind so as to accelerate the process of realization of fundamental unity.

*Young India*, 20-8-'25

## 26

## A CHRISTIAN LETTER

Rajkumari Amrit Kaur was with me during the Travancore pilgrimage. Though she could not enter the temples, she followed the pilgrimage in all other respects. She has felt moved by what she observed during the pilgrimage, and has placed in my hands the following letter which I dare not withhold from the reader:

> "My personal conviction of the error of a militant attitude on the part of any one religion towards another has been of long standing. So long ago as when I was 15 years of age I remember refusing to join in singing—though I was a member of the school choir—Bishop Heber's well-known hymn: 'From Greenland's Icy Mountains.' To me,

therefore, conversion or the desire to impel another person to change his faith has always savoured of an arrogance tantamount to a violent attitude of mind, which must surely be against that very doctrine of love for which I believe that Christ lived and died.

I am of opinion that the missionary, with the best intention in the world—for we must credit him with honesty of purpose—has wronged Indian Christians in more ways than one. Many converts here have been denationalized, e.g. even their names have been changed in many instances to those of Europeans; they have been told that there is no true light to be found in the religion of their forefathers. The ancient scriptures of their ancestors are a closed book to them. They have had implanted in them a psychology of fear in regard to their non-Christian brothers. How often have I not heard educated Christians saying that, if the British Raj were to be removed, the first people to suffer a wholesale massacre would be the Indian Christian community! The warring sects of the various Christian churches have each formed their own communities in India, with the result that the seed of those very dissensions which have been the cause of strife within the Christian Church in the West has been sown here regardless of the fact that this in itself was a stumbling block to the people whom they wished to convert to a 'better' religion. A woman member of my staff was sent by me once to worship in a non-conformist temple, and I cannot forget the rebuke she received later from the priest of her church for having committed a sin by this innocent action of hers! At the same time, while there has been no conscious effort to purge the Indian Church of the taint of untouchability that exists within its own doors, the untouchability that exists in Hinduism has been exploited to the extent of attempted mass and wholesale conversions to so-called Christianity of the Depressed Classes. I say 'so-called Christianity' advisedly, because I know that not one of these poor people to whom I have spoken—and I have spoken to many—has been able to tell me anything of the spiritual implications of his change of faith. That he is equally ignorant of the faith of his forefathers and has been sadly neglected by his own community, does not seem to me to be ample or any reason for transplanting him to an alien soil where he can find no root. I am one of those who firmly believe that the spiritually-minded intelligentsia of Indian Christians have to evolve for themselves a religion which will be purged of the many impurities which exist in institutional Christianity as it stands today, that they will have to purify their own hearts of the arrogance that denies salvation to all who do not happen to be labelled 'Christians', that they will have to strive to enshrine Jesus in the hearts of all their fellow-men by the radiance and joy of His continual presence in their own lives, that they will have to seek Him and worship Him in the lowliest of God's creation, by whatsoever religious label they are called.

Your utterances during your pilgrimage of penitence in Travancore have been a great joy. In particular do I rejoice in your special message to the Christian community at Kottayam. In admitting once again the equality of all religions you have given Christians much food for thought, and I hope and pray that this will be the beginning of an era of self-purification for them no less than for the members of the Hindu fold. Are we not all Hindus inasmuch as we are the children of Hind? Is there not room for Jesus in Hinduism? There must be. I cannot believe that any who seek to worship God in spirit and in truth are outside the pale of any of the great religions which draw their inspiration from Him who is the fountain-head of all Truth. I am sure I am not the only Indian born in the Christian faith who holds these views, but I feel that, if the teaching and example of Jesus are to enrich the life of our country, Indian Christians must turn the searchlight inwards and seek to serve in that spirit of humility and tolerance which is the essence of all true religion and without which there can be no unity and no peace and goodwill on earth.

Will you not help the Indian Christian to realize his mission? You can, because you have drawn inspiration from Jesus' undying teachings as embodied in the Sermon on the Mount. We assuredly stand in need of guidance."

Owing to her close contact with me there was hesitation on my part over the publication. But the knowledge that she has very imperfectly voiced what other Christian friends have told me has overcome my hesitation. But I do not feel competent to guide Indian Christians. I can, however, appeal to them as I did at Kottayam and as I have done before then through these columns. I am on safer ground in responding to the Rajkumari's belief that there is in Hinduism room enough for Jesus, as there is for Mahomed, Zoroaster and Moses. For me the different religions are beautiful flowers from the same garden, or they are branches of the same majestic tree. Therefore they are equally true, though being received and interpreted through human instruments equally imperfect. It is impossible for me to reconcile myself to the idea of conversion after the style that goes on in India and elsewhere today. It is an error which is perhaps the greatest impediment to the world's progress towards peace. 'Warring creeds' is a blasphemous expression. And it fitly describes the state of things in India, the mother—as I believe her to be—of Religion or religions. If she is truly the mother, the motherhood is on trial. Why should a Christian want to convert a Hindu to Christianity and vice versa? Why should he not be satisfied if the Hindu is a good or godly man? If the morals of a man is a matter of no concern, the form of worship in a particular manner in a church, a mosque or a temple is an empty formula, it may even be a hindrance to individual or social growth, and insistence on a particular form or repetition of a credo may be a potent cause of violent quarrels leading to bloodshed and ending in utter disbelief in Religion i.e. God Himself.

*Harijan*, 30-1-'37

## 27

## "OUR PARTIAL SIGHT"

The reader will remember Rajkumari Amrit Kaur's letter to me published in these columns some weeks ago. She received on it, some time ago, a letter from an English friend. She sent it to me to read. It contained so much that was good that I asked for permission to publish the relevant portion. This she readily gave and copied it for me. Here are the passages:

"I have been meaning to write to you ever since I read in *Harijan* your fine letter to Mr. Gandhi. I want to tell you how very much I feel with you about what you said with regard to missionary work and to thank you for saying it in your own way to a man like Mahatmaji. When I was in India, first as a very undeveloped girl thrust into a C. M. S. atmosphere, very many years ago, I felt that the approach of the missionaries to the people of India was all wrong and I had lonely times of being up against the whole system and yet not exactly being able to formulate my ideas or talk to others with any chance of being understood. I was also set wondering if we as British people had any right to be ruling India, and I remember expressing this in those early days and being firmly dealt with! ! But ever since those days as my thought life has developed I have been getting to feel that fundamentally the whole position of the British in India was wrong and that the missionaries as a whole were sharing in the superiority complex of those who ruled. I am regarded, I know, as a real black sheep in missionary circles. So I can thoroughly sympathize with criticism that I am sure you have met with from those quarters! But what you said needed saying by someone who was a Christian and who yet saw a different way of sharing her faith with others. And it makes all the difference when someone like you who is known and has a position in the country says these things.

We sing in our churches in England that grand hymn, whose words I expect you know, written by that inspired blind poet George Matheson:

'Gather us in; we worship only Thee
In varied names we stretch a common hand;
In diverse forms a common soul we see;
In many ships we seek one spirit land;
Gather us in.
Each sees one colour in thy rainbow light,
Each looks upon one tint and calls it heaven,
Thou art the fulness of our partial sight;
We are not perfect till we find the seven;
Gather us in.'

Anyway it is a step beyond 'From Greenland's icy mountains'! But I sometimes wonder if the people here who sing this realize its implications."

*Harijan*, 17-4-'37

28

## AN UNFORTUNATE DOCUMENT

Fourteen highly educated Indian Christians occupying important social positions have issued a joint manifesto setting forth their views on the missionary work among Harijans. The document has been published in the Indian Press. I was disinclined to publish it in *Harijan*, as after having read it more than once I could not bring myself to say anything in its favour and I felt that a critical review of it might serve no useful purpose. But I understand that my criticism is expected and will be welcomed no matter how candid and strong it may be.

[The following is the manifesto:]

### "OUR DUTY TO THE DEPRESSED AND BACKWARD CLASSES"

*An Indian Christian Statement*

As Indian Christians interested in the welfare of the country and the future of Christianity in the land, we feel called upon to give utterance to certain convictions which are forced upon us by the propaganda that is being carried on in this country and the West regarding the present so-called unparalleled opportunities for the spread of the Gospel among the Depressed and Backward classes in India, and the consequent misunderstanding that has arisen in the minds of non-Christians.

*Section I*

*Our Analysis of the Situation*

The general unrest in the country during the past century has contained a note of religious quest among the people of India from the highest to the lowest. But, due chiefly to the spread of nationalism, religious values seem to have receded into the background; and in such cases as the self-respect and certain forms of socialist movements they seem to have been discarded as anti-social and anti-national.

An arresting feature of the national upheaval is the spirit of revolt manifested by the leaders of the Depressed and Backward classes against the lot that was assigned to their people in the social, economic and religious fabric of Hindu Society for centuries and the large measures of sympathy with which their demand for drastic remedies for their desperate situation is being met by Hindu reformers. We cannot fail to note that these efforts have achieved a signal success in the great Temple Entry Proclamation made by the Ruler of what was reputed to be a conservative and orthodox Hindu State.

There has always been a dissatisfaction with the tyranny of caste among liberal-minded Hindus. But at the present moment the incentive to the removal of the age-long grievances of the Depressed and Backward classes comes more from nationalistic and humanitarian than from religious considerations. The nationally-minded Hindu, who regarded caste and untouchability as a blot on his civilization, and looked with sullen displeasure on the steady drifting of many members of these classes into other religious communities, was suddenly awakened to the immense danger lurking in this drift, especially by the communal basis on which the privileges of the new Constitution have been devised. Promoted by the feeling that the Indian Christian Community has, on the whole, remained outside the current of national effort and aspiration, the Hindu has come to regard any migration, large or small, from the Hindu to the Christian Community as a loss to the nation.

The entry of a political value into the realm of religion has had a two-fold consequence. In the first place, the Hindu can no longer look with equanimity upon conversions from Hinduism to other faiths, for they constitute a direct blow to his political strength. In the second place, one strand of worldly motives which may enter into and vitiate religious conversions has been eliminated inasmuch as the Depressed and Backward classes are better off within the Hindu fold than outside it. A sifting and testing of motives has begun to operate just now, and symptoms and signs of a movement from Hinduism to Islam or Christianity which were assessed so late as a year or even six months ago will have to be re-assessed, if indeed they continue to appear in anything like the strength in which they appeared then.

In view of the political complications that have got so inextricably mixed with the uprising of the Depressed and Backward classes and their desire for a fuller life, the redoubled enthusiasm of Muslims and Christian leaders to commend their religions to the acceptance of those people has naturally aroused the suspicion and resentment of Hindus. Communal animosities are therefore bound to be intensified in the near future. This is a prospect which no Christian in India can contemplate with indifference. The danger present in this situation need not be emphasized. But it is necessary to point out that herein the Christian with a true missionary motive has the opportunity to conserve all that is conducive to national unity and depth of spirituality.

*Section II*

*Convictions and Conclusions*

The above analysis, which we believe will appear correct to all who have watched the movement among the Depressed and Backward classes and the sudden impetus it has received from the promulgation of the Indian Constitution, has brought to us these convictions and lead us to these conclusions:

1. We sympathize with the Depressed and Backward classes in their struggle to secure for themselves a fuller life and rejoice with them and Hindu reformers over the success that has attended their combined efforts at social and economic uplift and over the fact of their having won full recognition of the principles of religious equality in Travancore. We trust that they will gain further successes in these directions.

2. We believe that the process of absorption of the Depressed and Backward classes into the Hindu community, in which a serious beginning has been made, is likely to confer on the present generation of the Depressed and Backward classes immediate benefits on a large scale which the Church will not be able to give to the whole community.

3. We are of opinion that with the political privileges which the Indian Constitution and the Poona Pact have conferred on these classes, with the special educational and other advantages provided in many Indian Provinces for their exclusive uplift, and with this great gesture of friendliness which the Caste Hindus have shown them, they will not have the same dissatisfaction with Hinduism which often times led them to gravitate towards Christianity or Islam. Therefore we are unable to share the hope

that the present upheaval is going to result in an influx of the Depressed and Backward classes into the Christian Church in the phenomenal measure in which, it is said, it is going to happen.

4. We believe that the Christian Church in India should welcome this movement not only as a laudable effort to expel from Hinduism an out-of-date and unholy institution but as a reform which is bound to have a wholesome effect on the entire social structure of India including the Indian Church, by solving the problem of caste prejudices in the home of their origin. We believe that this is certainly an effective way in which caste which has proved itself such an insidious danger to the Christian Church also can be most successfully overcome.

5. In our view there is an obvious danger in any propaganda by Christians in which the religious element of the unrest is stressed, to the extent of obscuring its real nature as a social upheaval. An aggressive evangelistic programme formulated in these circumstances will, besides being misunderstood as an exploitation of the difficulties of the Hindus, result in undermining any attempt at concerted action on the part of all communities so necessary for the success of this great endeavour towards social justice.

6. Mass Conversions, from the point of view of the Depressed and Backward classes, were in the past mainly the outcome of the desire for social justice and all-round uplift, and the Christian Church has succeeded in helping large sections of converts from these communities to a higher standard of life—social, economic, moral and spiritual—and to real transformation in the life and character of individuals and groups belonging to these classes. Further, these results have provoked the serious thought and attention of the privileged classes to the claims and aspirations of the Depressed and Backward classes. We have, however, to recognize that these mass conversions have generally

lowered Christian standards so badly as to have left for the Indian Church a legacy of deplorable caste prejudices and jealousies, on account of which its progress, solidarity and its proclaimed witness to the oneness of all humanity in Christ Jesus suffer not a little even to this day.

7. We recognize that in an atmosphere free from the heat and dust of the present upheaval and apart from all political considerations, Christianity will continue to exercise the attraction which it has always had for the poor of the land and others in whom a hunger for the things of the spirit has been awakened. Men and women, individually and in family or village groups, will continue to seek the fellowship of the Christian Church. That is the real movement of the Spirit of God. And no power on earth can stem that tide. It will be the duty of the Christian Church in India to receive such seekers after the truth as it is in Jesus Christ and provide for them instruction and spiritual nurture. The Church will cling to its right to receive such people into itself from whatever religious group they may come. It will cling to the further right to go about in these days of irreligion and materialism to awaken spiritual hunger in all.

Indian public men shall have to concede, as indeed they have done in the Karachi Congress Resolutions, to all religious groups the right not only to profess and practise, but also to propagate, their religions. And in view of what Christianity has done to those who have entered the Church and to the whole of the country as a moral force and spiritual leaven, they would not want to curtail its freedom to continue to render this unique service.

8. We are convinced that the Gospel of Jesus is a Gospel not only to the poor and down-trodden masses in India but to all sections of the country's population, and that the task before the Indian Church is to permeate the ideology and outlook of the land with a genuine respect for

the teachings of Jesus and a willingness to accept His leadership in all that concerns personal happiness and national well-being. The service that it can render to the Depressed and Backward classes and its own development in membership as well as in spirituality should form part of this larger programme. We recognize with thankfulness that this larger task of evangelization, unaffected by economic and political upheavals, has been and is going on. Therefore we deem it very unwise at this juncture to alienate the sympathy and spoil the open-mindedness of the Hindu to the Gospel by any ill-considered attempts at external results of a questionable value. The Indian Church by availing itself of the present opportunity to show that it is one with the rest of the people of the land in its desire to support every good cause that makes for economic uplift, social justice, national solidarity and genuine spirituality, should disarm suspicion and win for itself recognition as a national asset in the best sense of the term. Thus and thus only it can augment the leavening process which is also an important task of the Church and commend the Gospel to the whole of India.

K. K. Chandy, B. A., Sevak, Christavasram, Alleppey.
S. Gnanaprakasam, B. A., Coimbatore.
S. Gurubatham, Doctor, Mission Hospital, Coimbatore.
S. Jesudasen, F. R. C. S., Sevak, Christukulashram, Tirupattur.
M. P. Job, B. A., L. T., Sevak, Christavasram, Alleppey.
G. V. Job, M. A., L. T., St. Columbia's High School, Chingleput.
G. Joseph, Doctor, Eye Hospital, Trichinopoly.
K. I. Matthai, B. A., Sevak, Christavasram, Alleppey.
A. A. Paul, B. A., International Fellowship, Madras.
S. E. Runganadham, M. A., Diwan Bahadur, Ex-Vice-Chancellor, Annamalai University, Madras.
A. N. Sudarisanam, B. A., Editor, *The Guardian*, Madras.

O. F. E. Zacharias, B. A., L. T., Madras Christian College, Madras; Hon. Secretary, Indian Christian Association, Madras.

D. M. Devasahayam, B. A., B. D., Nagercoil.

G. Y. Martyn, M. A., Up-Acharya, Christa Prema Seva Sangh Ashram, Poona.

*N. B.* Those who have signed have done it in their personal capacity.

The authors seem to have fallen between two stools in their attempt to sit on both. They have tried to reconcile the irreconcilable. If one section of Christians has been aggressively open and militant, the other represented by the authors of the manifesto is courteously patronizing. They would not be aggressive for the sake of expedience. The purpose of the manifesto is not to condemn unequivocally the method of converting the illiterate and the ignorant but to assert the right of preaching the Gospel to the millions of Harijans. The key to the manifesto is contained in paragraphs 7 and 8. This is what one reads in paragraph 7: "Men and women individually and in family or village groups will continue to seek the fellowship of the Christian Church. That is the real movement of the Spirit of God. And no power on earth can stem that tide. It will be the duty of the Christian Church in India to receive such seekers after the truth as it is in Jesus Christ and provide for them instruction and spiritual nurture. The Church will cling to its right to receive such people into itself from whatever religious group they may come. It will cling to the further right to go about in these days of irreligion and materialism to awaken spiritual hunger in all." These few sentences are a striking instance of how the wish becomes father to the thought. It is an unconscious process but not on that account less open to criticism. Men and women do not seek the fellowship of the Christian Church. Poor Harijans are no better than the others. I wish they had real spiritual hunger. Such as it is, they satisfy by visits to the temples, however crude they may be. When the missionary of another religion goes to them, he goes like any vendor of goods. He has no special spiritual merit that will distinguish him from those to whom he goes. He does, however, possess material goods which he promises to those who will come to his fold. Then mark, the duty of Christian Church in India turns into a right. Now when duty becomes a right it ceases to be a duty. Performance of a duty requires one quality—that of suffering and introspection. Exercise of a right requires a quality that gives the power to impose one's will upon the resister through sanctions devised by the claimant or the law whose aid he invokes in the exercise of his right. I have the duty of paying my debt, but I have no right to thrust the owed coppers (say) into the pocket of an unwilling creditor. The duty of taking spiritual message is performed by the messenger becoming a fit vehicle by prayer and fasting. Conceived as a right, it may easily become an imposition on unwilling parties.

Thus the manifesto, undoubtedly designed to allay suspicion and soothe the ruffled feelings of Hindus, in my opinion fails to accomplish its purpose. On the contrary it leaves a bad taste in the mouth. I venture to suggest to the authors that they need to re-examine their position in the light of my remarks. Let them recognize the fundamental difference between rights and duties. In the spiritual sphere, there is no such thing as a right.

*Harijan*, 3-4-'37

## 29

## FOUR QUESTIONS

A correspondent asks the following four questions:

"1. Hindus who once renounced their faith for some reason or other and joined Islam or Christianity, sincerely repent and want to come back. Should we re-convert them or not? You may take the instance of your own son Harilal.

2. Lakhs of the Depressed Class people in South India, as you know, have joined Christianity wholesale. Some of them, since the Travancore Durbar's Declaration and the popularity of the Harijan movement, feel it worth while to readopt their ancestral faith. What would you advise about them?

3. A Hindu was made to join another faith for certain material considerations. After some time he feels disillusioned and comes and knocks at our door. Shall we welcome him or not?

4. Young Hindu boys and girls are often taken hold of by Christian missionaries and converted. At some places Muslims are also making use of their orphanages for this purpose. What should we do, when these boys and girls, either alone or with their guardians, approach us for *Shuddhi*?"

These, or such questions have been asked and answered before now in these columns in some shape or other. I do not need to answer each separately. In my opinion they are not examples of real heart conversions. If a person, through fear, compulsion, starvation or for material gain or consideration, goes over to another faith, it is a misnomer to call it conversion. Most cases of mass conversions, of which we have heard so much during the past two years, have been to my mind false coin. Real conversion springs from the heart and at the prompting of God, not of a stranger. The voice of God can always be distinguished from the voice of man. The hypothetical cases coined by my correspondent are, so far as I can see, not cases of conversion. I would, therefore, unhesitatingly readmit to the Hindu fold all such repentants without ado, certainly without any *Shuddhi*. *Shuddhi* is not applicable to such cases. And, as I believe in the equality of all the great religions of the earth, I regard no man as polluted because he has forsaken the branch on which he was sitting and gone over to another of the same tree. If he comes back to the original branch, he deserves to be welcomed and not told that he had committed a sin by reason of his having forsaken the family to which he belonged. In so far as he may be deemed to have erred, he has sufficiently purged himself of it when he repents of the error and retraces his step.

***Harijan*, 25-9-'37**

## 30

## CONVERSION WITHOUT CONVICTION

*Q*. You oppose all conversion without conviction. But are you not inconsistent? You profess equal respect for all religions. Why then worry about how the conversion is brought about?

*A*. I have extracted the question from your long and plausible letter, cleverly written. Conversion without conviction is a mere change and not conversion, which is a revolution in one's life. You seem too to forget that equal respect implies respect for my own faith as much as for yours or any other neighbour's. My respect for my own faith forbids my being indifferent to my children abandoning their parents' faith without conviction. And I should have little respect for you if you led my children astray by making all kinds of worldly promises in which matters of the spirit had no play.

***Harijan*, 29-3-'42**

31

## WHAT IS NEUTRALITY

An American missionary writes:

"Although we have never met I have been a reader of your paper *Harijan* and have given a good deal of thought to your ideas. I think your stand for non-violence is very good. In that you certainly set a good example to Christians. And I believe that is according to the teachings of Christ. Certainly Christ taught non-violence when he taught returning good for evil and turning the other cheek, and going two miles with anyone who compelled you to go one mile. You as a Mahatma must admire such teachings of Christ.

But I must ask you a question. Are you and the Congress generally neutral in regard to which religion a person belongs to? I believe the Congress claim to be neutral, but my contention is that they are not.

Your friend, the late prime minister of Madras, sent a wire of congratulation to Christians who became Hindus. Is that being neutral? And just the other day, here near Bombay in Thana District, when about fifty hill people returned to Hinduism, the leaders in making them Hindus were the Congress leaders of Thana District. So this plainly shows that the Congress leaders favour Hinduism.

Under such a Government what chance would the small minority of Christians stand when Purna Swaraj is given to be monopolized by the Hindu majority? No doubt, independence should be given to India, but what no one except the Hindus wants is a Hindu raj. For, the poor Christians left to the mercy of some anti-Christian leaders are not likely to fare very well.

In all that you have sought to do during your long life for the benefit of India, you no doubt have the sympathy and good wishes of all good Christian missionaries. But we must naturally consider the welfare of nearly seven millions of Christians in this land. Are they to be placed at the mercy of anti-Christian leaders? Will it be possible for the Congress Government to be impartial and neutral in religious matters as the British Government has been? If not, we certainly would not hail it as a blessing."

I am not aware of what Shri Rajagopalachari said. He is well able to take care of himself. But I can give my idea of neutrality. In free India every religion should prosper on terms of equality, unlike what is happening today. Christianity being the nominal religion of the rulers, it receives favours which no other religion enjoys. A Government responsible to the people dare not favour one religion over another. But I should see nothing wrong in Hindus congratulating those who having left them may return to their fold. I think that the Christians of free America would rejoice at the return to their ancestral Christianity of Americans of the slums—if there are any in America—temporarily calling themselves Hindus under the influence of a plausible Hindu missionary. I have already complained of the methods adopted by some missionaries to wean ignorant people from the religion of their forefathers. It is one thing to preach one's religion to whomsoever may choose to adopt it, another to entice masses. And if those thus enticed, on being undeceived, go back to their old love, their return will give natural joy to those whom they had forsaken. The missionary friend errs in regarding the Congress as a Hindu organization. It has on its roll perhaps three million men and women. Its register is open to all. As a matter of fact it has on it men and women belonging to all religions. There is no reason why Christians or Muslims should not capture the Congress. It is true, however, that a national democratic Government will represent the majority of Hindu voters in the aggregate. But owing to unequal distribution of population in the various provinces, Bengal, Punjab, Frontier and Sind have a preponderance of Muslims, as the other provinces of Hindus.

I hold that it is wrong to look at the question from the narrow sectarian standpoint. The only true standpoint is national. Therefore the American missionary seems to me to labour under a threefold mistake when he mistakes a natural joy for want of neutrality, regards the Congress as a Hindu organization, and views India as divided religiously into parts hostile to and suspicious of one another. But economic and political aspirations of all the communities are surely the same except that the privileged ones will find their privileges melting in the sunshine of freedom. It seems to me to be wrong to import religious differences into a political discussion. Common law should prevent any injustice.

Sevagram, 24-12-'39

*Harijan*, 30-12-'39

## 32

## UNTOUCHABILITY AND CONVERSION

*Q.* If the object of the Congress in the liquidation of untouchability is to give Harijans a status of equality with the rest, is this not achieved by their conversion to Islam? Why does the Independence Pledge allocate the programme of the removal of untouchability to the Hindus only? Does this not show that the Congress is anxious to maintain a Hindu majority and therefore denies to the Mussalmans their right of conversion?

*A.* Liquidation of untouchability cannot be attained by the conversion of untouchables to Islam or any other religion. For it is the so-called Caste Hindu who has to rid himself of the sin of untouchability. He can wash away the stain only by doing justice, however tardy, to the outcaste. You will thus see why Muslims are not invited by the Congress to share the burden with the Hindus. They have committed no sin against the untouchables. I cannot prevent you from looking at a simple but necessary social reform as a political dodge to maintain a majority. Tens of thousands of Hindus who are doing penance have no thought of majority. All they want is to do justice to those whom, under the guise of religion, Caste Hindus have reduced to a state worse than slavery. Lastly, you are hopelessly wrong in suggesting that the Congress denies the right to Muslims to convert 'untouchables'. The Congress cannot prevent anybody from doing conversion work. Whether you will exercise the right in the right manner or wrong is for you to consider.

Sevagram, 15-4-'40

*Harijan*, 20-4-'40

# CHRISTIAN MISSIONS

THEIR PLACE IN INDIA

## PART II

## REPORTS OF SPEECHES AND CONVERSATIONS

## 1

## THE RELIGIOUS PROBLEM

Pierre Ceresole and Joe Wilkinson both belong to that true type of a missionary whose mission is the noble one of selfless service of humanity. 'One of the noblest missionaries I met was—who said to me that he had converted only one man during fourteen years and that too in spite of himself,' said Ceresole. And he proceeded to tell Gandhiji of some of the books he had recently read. There was *India in the Dark Wood* offering the orthodox Protestant solution of salvation through Christ, wanting 'the main framework of the dominant Hindu philosophy to be shattered.' 'India can only recover under the guidance of Christ Jesus,' repeats the author over and again, and Pierre Ceresole said he had turned from this book with relief to Frank Lenwood's book *Jesus—Lord or Leader* where the author rejects the claim of Christianity as the final religion and pines for 'a fuller and richer faith than we have yet reached and to believe that God, who has nowhere left Himself without witness, will use the highest intuitions of other systems and of many races to enrich the thinking and worship of mankind.' He sees definite gain in the abandonment of a special claim for the inspiration of the Bible, and classes himself among those 'who humbly desire to follow Jesus as leader, though their view of truth will not allow them to worship him as Lord.'

'There is a swing in the pendulum,' said Gandhiji, 'and I have a Christian friend telling me that the Gita shows him how to live the New Testament, and that many passages in the latter which used to be dark were intelligible to him through a study of the Gita.'

And yet Ceresole feels that each one must find his solace from his own faith. He attended our prayer meetings regularly, morning and evening, but said one evening: 'This repetition of one and the same thing over and over again jars on me. It may be the defect of my rationalist mathematical temperament. But somehow I cannot like the repetition. For instance even Bach's wonderful music fails to appeal to me when the text 'Father, forgive them, they know not what they do,' is repeated over and over again.'

'But even in mathematics you have your recurring decimals,' said Gandhiji smiling.

'But each recurs with a definite new fact,' said the mathematician.

'Even so,' said Gandhiji, 'each repetition, or *japa* as it is called, has a new meaning, each repetition carries you nearer and nearer to God. This is a concrete fact, and I may tell you that you are here talking to no theorist but to one who has experienced what he says every minute of his life, so much so that it is easier for the life to stop than for this incessant process to stop. It is a definite need of the soul.'

'I quite see it, but for the average man it becomes an empty formula.'

'I agree, but the best thing is liable to be abused. There is room for any amount of hypocrisy, but even hypocrisy is an ode to virtue. And I know that for ten thousand hypocrites you would find millions of simple souls who find their solace from it. It is like scaffolding quite essential to a building.'

'But,' said Pierre Ceresole, 'if I may carry the simile a little further, you agree that the scaffolding has to be removed when the building is complete?'

'Yes, it would be removed when this body is removed.'

'Why?'

'Because,' said Wilkinson who was closely following the discourse, 'we are eternally building.'

'Because,' said Gandhiji, 'we are eternally striving after perfection. God alone is perfect, man is never perfect.'

* * *

A Christian student, who is now with us studying things and preparing to qualify himself for village work, asked Gandhiji whether there could be any service without religion.

'Why,' said Gandhiji, 'service which has not the slightest touch of self in it is itself the highest religion.'

'But one must be devoted to someone?'

'Yes, to Truth. I am devoted to none but Truth and I owe no discipline to anybody but Truth.'

'But how is one to get inspiration from this general idea?'

'That means to say that you want a God who has form, Truth is too impersonal for you? Well, idolatry is embedded in human nature. But you may, if you like, worship God as Truth, if not Truth as God. God is Truth, but God is many other things also. That is why I prefer to say Truth is God. But you need not go into what may sound like mystic lore; you may simply worship what you find to be the Truth, for Truth is known relatively. Only remember that Truth is not one of the many qualities that we name. It is the living embodiment of God, it is the only Life, and I identify Truth with fullest life, and that is how it becomes a concrete thing, for God is His whole creation, the whole Existence, and service of all that exists—Truth—is service of God.'

'But how should we Christian students go to the villagers? They might shun us because we are Christians.'

'You will tell them: "We are Christians, but don't be alarmed, even as we are not alarmed because you are Hindus. We have no design on you, as we know that you have no design on us. We want you to be better Hindus, even as by reason of our contact with you we know that we will be better Christians." That is the way of approach. It is idle to talk of winning souls for God. Is God so helpless that He cannot win souls for Himself? Everyone's religion is a personal matter with himself. I cannot preach Hinduism, I can but practise it.'

*Harijan*, 25-5-'35 M. D.

## 2

## IS RELIGIOUS UNITY POSSIBLE?

Dr. Rahm from Switzerland was perplexed by the many warring creeds in the world and wondered if there was no way of ending the conflict.

'It depends on Christians,' said Gandhiji. 'If only they would make up their minds to unite with the others! But they will not do so. Their solution is universal acceptance of Christianity as they believe it. An English friend has been at me for the past thirty years trying to persuade me that there is nothing but damnation in Hinduism and that I must accept Christianity. When I was in jail I got, from separate sources, no less than three copies of *The Life of Sister Therese*, in the hope that I should follow her example and accept Jesus as the only begotten son of God and my Saviour. I read the book prayerfully but I could not accept even St. Therese's testimony for myself. I must say I have an open mind, if indeed at this stage and age of my life I can be said to have an open mind on this question. Anyway I claim to have an open mind in this sense that, if things were to happen to me as they did to Saul before he became Paul, I should not hesitate to be converted.

'But today I rebel against orthodox Christianity, as I am convinced that it has distorted the message of Jesus. He was an Asiatic whose message was delivered through many media, and when it had the backing of a Roman Emperor it became an imperialist faith as it remains to this day. Of course there are noble but rare exceptions like Andrews and Elwin. But the general trend is as I have indicated.

'There was held the other day in Bombay a parliament of religions. Now a positive bar to a real parliament of religions is the refusal to accept an equal basis and a mutual regard for one another's faith. We must not forget that it is a parliament of *religions*, and not of a few religious-minded men. Did Christianity enter the parliament on a par with the others?'

*Harijan*, 30-5-'36 M. D.

## 3

## WITH MISSIONARY FRIENDS

Among the new missionary friends is a Danish couple, Mr. and Mrs. Bjerrum, full of sympathy and eagerness to establish an understanding between themselves and those whom they serve. After giving their pleasant impressions of the Exhibition, Mr. Bjerrum began to talk of the students of his college. 'The dress of most of our students is Europeanized,' he informed Gandhiji not without some sorrow. 'It is a great pity,' said Gandhiji, 'that Christianity should be mixed up with foreign dress and foreign ways of eating and drinking.' 'It is indeed,' chimed in Mrs. Bjerrum. 'But don't you think a change has already begun?' 'Well,' replied Gandhiji, 'a change in thought is certainly coming over, but not a corresponding change in conduct,' and with this he narrated some of his experiences with the friends of the Y. M. C. A. of Calcutta. 'May we know,' asked Mr. Bjerrum, 'what form in your opinion missionary work should take if the missionaries are to stay in India?' 'Yes. They have to alter their attitude. Today they tell people that there is no salvation for them except through the Bible and through Christianity. It is customary to decry other religions and to offer their own as the only one that can bring deliverance. That attitude should be radically changed. Let them appear before the people as they are, and try to rejoice in seeing Hindus become better Hindus and Mussalmans better Mussalmans. Let them start work at the bottom, let them enter into what is best in their life and offer nothing inconsistent with it. That will make their work far more efficacious, and what they will say and offer to the people will be appreciated without suspicion and hostility. In a word, let them go to the people not as patrons but as one of them, not to oblige them but to serve them and to work among them.'

'Thank you. We are going to Denmark next year and would like to take some message from you.'

'Well, I have given you my message.'

'That we will deliver, but something in particular for our people.'

'The external is always an expression of the internal, and if the people of Denmark would serve us, let them teach us their life-giving industry of co-operative dairy and cattle-breeding.'

Gandhiji invited them to go and spend a few days at the Ashram before leaving for home, and they gratefully accepted the invitation.

*Young India*, 14-7-'27 M. D.

## 4

## TALKS WITH MISSIONARIES

*The Art of Ministry*

There were two little talks during the last week with the members of the Christian faith, some of them would-be missionaries and others missionaries. The first was at the United Theological College, Bangalore. There was no discussion here, but the motto of the College, 'Go ye not to be ministered unto, but to minister unto other people,' served as the text of the little talk that Gandhiji gave. The first desideratum, he said, was a knowledge of Hindi for those who aspired to be ministers to the masses of the country. 'I confess,' he said, 'that it is the fault of the previous generation who committed us to the medium of English. But you must break the barrier, if you would reach the masses beyond the Vindhya range. As regards the service that can be or should be rendered by you, I don't think I need speak much, for you have made my task easy by endorsing my mission of the spinning wheel. You have mentioned the depressed classes, but there is a vast mass of men who are more depressed than the so-called depressed classes, and who constitute the real India. The vast network of railways touches but a fringe of these masses, and if you will travel somewhat outside the railway beat, you will visualize them. These railway lines running north to south and east to west are arteries which drain away the wealth of the masses,—Lord Salisbury used the word 'bleed',—and no return is made to them. We in the cities become partners in the blood-sucking process—which phrase, however bad it may be, truly depicts the state of things. I have known something of this class. I have brooded over their wants, and if I was a painter I could draw a picture of them with their blank eyes, without a spark of lustre or life in them. How are we to minister to them? Tolstoy gave the picturesque phrase, 'Let us get off the shoulders of our neighbours.' If everyone performs that single operation, he would have rendered all service God requires of him. It is a startling proposition, and as you are in a place where you are learning the art of ministry, you must work it out. Build up the premises one on another and see what you arrive at. If you discover any other method than I have suggested of getting off the backs of those poor people, let me know. I am a learner myself, I have no axe to grind, and wherever I see a truth I take it up and try to act up to it.

'A missionary friend from America wrote to me suggesting literary education for the masses instead of the Charkha. Well, I felt sorry for him, especially because he had written the letter from the fulness of his heart. I do not think even Jesus knew much of letters, and if the early Christians cultivated literary knowledge, it was in order to perform their ministry better. But I suppose there is no passage in the New Testament in which there is even the slightest emphasis placed on mere literary education as the first condition for people to come to their own. Not that I discount literacy. It is a question of emphasis. It is like a good thing misplaced just like matter which misplaced becomes dirt. And whenever I see wrong emphasis being placed on a good thing, my soul rises up against it. Before a child has knowledge of letters, it must be fed and clothed and taught the art of feeding itself. I do not want it to be spoon-fed, but self-reliant. Let our children first know the use of their hands and feet. So I say the first condition is to take to them the message of the spinning wheel.

'I did not like the expression 'patronizing Khadi' used by you. It has a bad odour. Will you become patrons or servants? So long as Khadi is patronized it will be a fad or fashion, but when it becomes a passion it will be the symbol of service. The moment you begin to use Khadi, you begin to serve. During my 35 years' constant contact with the poor I have found the art of service incredibly simple. It is not learnt in colleges and schools. The spirit of service can be learnt anywhere. Again here it is a question of emphasis. The art itself is as simple as the process whereby Saul became Paul. The change came over him with a flash, and immediately there is a change of heart in you, you become ministers. May God help to clear this for you.'

*Re-read the Bible*

The second was a talk as well as a discussion with the missionaries of Bangalore. Whereas the first was an appeal to them to take up his work, the second was an attempt to offer a corrective to their attitude towards the people they claimed to serve. Gandhiji opened the discussion by claiming himself to be a friend of the missionaries, ever since his close contact with them in South Africa. 'Though I have been a friend, I have always been a critic, not from any desire to be critical, but because I have felt that I would be a better friend if I opened out my heart, even at the risk of wounding their feelings. They never allowed me to think that they felt hurt, they certainly never resented my criticism.' Then he referred to his first speech before the missionaries in India on Swadeshi, since which twelve years had rolled away and with them much of the mists also.

'The first distinction I would like to make, after these prefatory remarks, between your missionary work and mine, is that while I am strengthening the faith of the people, you are undermining it. Your work, I have always held, will be all the richer if you accept as settled facts the faiths of the people you come to serve,—faiths which, however crude, are valuable to them. And in order to appreciate what I say, it becomes perhaps necessary to re-read the message of the Bible in terms of what is happening around us. The word is the same, but the spirit ever broadens intensively and extensively, and it might be that many things in the Bible will have to be re-interpreted in the light of discoveries—not of modern science—but in the spiritual world in the shape of direct experiences common to all faiths. The fundamental verses of St. John do require to be re-read and re-interpreted. I have come to feel that like us human beings words have their evolution from stage to stage in the contents they hold. For instance the contents of the richest word—God—are not the same to every one of us. They will vary with experience of each. They will mean one thing to the Santhal and another to his next door neighbour Rabindranath Tagore. The Sanatanist may reject my interpretation of God and Hinduism. But God Himself is a long-suffering God who puts up with any amount of abuse and misinterpretations. If we were to put the spiritual experiences together, we would find a resultant which would answer the cravings of human nature. Christianity is 1900 years old, Islam is 1300 years old; who knows the possibility of either? I have not read the Vedas in the original, but have tried to assimilate their spirit and have not hesitated to say that, though the Vedas may be 13,000 years old,—or even a million years old, as they well may be, for the word of God is as old as God Himself,—even the Vedas must be interpreted in the light of our experience. The powers of God should not be limited by the limitations of our understanding. To you who have come to teach India, I therefore say, you cannot give without taking. If you have come to give rich treasures of experiences, open your hearts out to receive the treasures of this land, and you will not be disappointed, neither will you have misread the message of the Bible.'

Interesting questions and answers followed, which I summarize below:

*Q.* What then are we doing? Are we doing the right thing?

*A.* You are trying to do the right thing in the wrong way. I want you to complement the faith of the people instead of undermining it. As the Dewan of Mysore said in his address to the Assembly, the Adi Karnatakas should be made better Hindus, as they belong to Hinduism. I would similarly say to you, make us better Hindus, i.e. better men or women. Why should a man, even if he becomes a Christian, be torn from his surroundings? Whilst a boy I heard it being said that to become a Christian was to have a brandy bottle in one hand and beef in the other. Things are better now, but it is not unusual to find Christianity synonymous with denationalization and Europeanization. Must we give up our simplicity to become better people? Do not lay the axe at our simplicity.

*Q.* There are not only two issues before us, viz. to serve and to teach; there is a third issue, viz. evangelizing, declaring the glad tidings of the coming of Jesus and his death in redemption for our sins. What is the right way of giving the good news? We need not undermine the faith, but we may make people lose their faith in lesser things.

*A.* That lands me into the region of interpretation. Whilst I must not enter into it, I may suggest that God did not bear the Cross only 1900 years ago, but He bears it today. It would be poor comfort to the world if it had to depend upon a historical God who died 2,000 years ago. Do not then preach the God of history, but show Him as He lives today through you. In South Africa I met a number of friends, and read a number of books—Pearson, Parker and Butler—all giving their own interpretations, and I said to myself I must not bother myself with these conflicting interpretations. It is better to allow our lives to speak for us than our words. C. F. Andrews never preaches. He is incessantly doing his work. He finds enough work and stays where he finds it and takes no credit for bearing the Cross. I have the honour to know hundreds of honest Christians, but I have not known one better than Andrews.

*Q.* But what about animistic beliefs? Should they not be corrected?

*A.* Well, we have been working amongst the so-called untouchables and backward classes, and we have never bothered ourselves with their beliefs, animistic or otherwise. Superstitions and undesirable things go as soon as we begin to live the correct life. I concern myself not with their belief but with asking them to do the right thing. As soon as they do it, their belief rights itself.

*Q.* You speak of simplicity. But what are we to do in this age of motor cars? You could not have come here without a motor car!

*A.* Well, a motor car is not a necessity. I certainly did not need it to come here. If God wants you to be useful, He should find the means to make you useful. Motor cars do not mean the sum of our spiritual experience. There was no motor car in Jesus' or Muhammad's time, and yet they did not need them for their work. I do not hold them to be essential for real progress. We need to be humble. And humility and simplicity are not mere outward expressions. When Paul speaks of humility he means heart-humility. A true Christian has little need to speak. He goes about his Father's business. May I cite my own case? Speeches were the least part of my work in South Africa. Most of the 16,000 people who rose like one man and joined me had not even seen me, much less heard me speak.

*Q.* How can we help condemning if we feel that our Christian truth is the only reality?

*A.* That brings me to the duty of tolerance. If you cannot feel that the other faith is as true as yours, you should feel at least that the men are as true as you. The intolerance of the Christian missionaries does not, I am glad to say, take the ugly shape it used to take some years ago. Think of the caricature of Hinduism, which one finds in so many publications of the Christian Literature Society. A lady wrote to me the other day saying that unless I embraced Christianity all my work would be nothing worth. And of course that Christianity must mean what she understands as such! Well, all I can say is that it is a wrong attitude.

*Young India*, 11-8-'27 M. D.

5

## INTERESTING QUESTIONS

One of our missionary visitors put a number of interesting questions.

'You have the reputation of never being angry. Is that true?'

'It is not that I do not get angry. I do not give vent to anger. I cultivate the quality of patience as angerlessness, and generally speaking I succeed. But I only control my anger when it comes. How I find it possible to control it would be a useless question, for it is a habit that everyone must cultivate and must succeed in forming by constant practice.'

'When did you come to experience this great love for the poor? Could you tell me the period or the occasion?'

'I have always had a love for the poor all my life and in abundance. I could cite illustrations after illustrations from my past life to show that it was something innate in me. I have never felt that there was any difference between the poor and me. I have always felt toward them as my own kith and kin.'

'Don't you have anything like antipathy for filth and dirt?' The question was not unusual, coming as it did from a nurse of several years' experience.

'I have no antipathy against dirty people,' said Gandhiji, 'but I have a horror of dirt. I should not eat out of a dirty plate nor touch a dirty spoon or kerchief. But I believe in removing dirt to its proper place, where it ceases to be dirt.'

The visitor next discussed the question of beggary. 'I do feel,' said Gandhiji, 'that whilst it is bad to encourage begging, I will not send away a beggar without offering him work and food. If he does not work, I shall let him go without food. Those who are physically disabled like the halt and the maimed and the blind have got to be supported by the State. There is, however, a lot of fraud going on under cover of pretended blindness or even genuine blindness. So many blind have become rich because of ill-gotten gains. It would be a good thing if they were taken to an asylum, rather than be exposed to this temptation.'

Last came the question of questions which missionary friends are not tired of asking and Gandhiji is not tired of answering. 'You would prevent missionaries coming to India in order to baptize?'

'Who am I to prevent them? If I had power and could legislate, I should certainly stop all proselytizing. It is the cause of much avoidable conflict between classes and unnecessary heart-burning among missionaries. But I should welcome people of any nationality if they came to serve here for the sake of service. In Hindu households the advent of a missionary has meant the disruption of the family coming in the wake of change of dress, manners, language, food and drink.'

'Is it not the old conception you are referring to? No such thing is now associated with proselytization.'

'The outward condition has perhaps changed, but the inward mostly remains. Vilification of Hindu religion, though subdued, is there. If there was a radical change in the missionaries' outlook would Murdoch's books be allowed to be sold in mission depots? Are those books prohibited by missionary societies? There is nothing but vilification of Hinduism in those books. You talk of the conception being no longer there. Only the other day a missionary descended on a famine area with money in his pocket, distributed it among the famine-stricken, converted them to his fold, took charge of their temple, and demolished it. This is outrageous. The temple could not belong to the converted Hindus, and it could not belong to the Christian missionary. But this friend goes and gets it demolished at the hands of the very men who only a little while ago believed that God was there.'

The lady seemed to be touched. Perhaps she had not heard of the incident. She said, 'In our hospital we do not try to influence our patients in their religious beliefs. Our doctor says we should not take an undue advantage of people in distress coming to us for treatment. But, Mr. Gandhi, why do you object to proselytization as such? Is not there enough in the Bible to authorize us to invite people to a better way of life?'

'Oh yes, but it does not mean that they should be made members of the Church. If you interpret your texts in the way you seem to do, you straightaway condemn a large part of humanity unless it believes as you do. If Jesus came to earth again, he would disown many things that are being done in the name of Christianity. It is not he who says 'Lord, Lord' that is a Christian, but 'He that doeth the will of the Lord' that is a true Christian. And cannot he who has not heard the name of Christ Jesus do the will of the Lord?'

*Harijan*, 11-5-'35 M. D.

## 6

## A STRANGE SEEKER

Prof. Krzenski from Poland was a rather strange specimen of a seeker of truth that I came across the other day. He said to Gandhiji that he had found much spirituality in India, and was wondering if all the spiritual forces of the world could not combine to conquer the materialistic forces that were gathering strong in India. But Catholicism, according to him, is the only true religion, and the only spiritual force. As a professor of philosophy he had studied all the religious systems of the world and had come to this deliberate conclusion!

"Do you therefore say that other religions are untrue?" Gandhiji asked him.

"If others are convinced that their religions are true, they are saved," said the professor, meaning to say that that conviction was impossible!

"Therefore," said Gandhiji, "you will say that everyone would be saved even through untruth. For you say that, if a man really and sincerely believes in what is as a matter of fact untruth, he is saved. Would you not also hold, therefore, that your own way may be untrue but that you are convinced that it is true and therefore you will be saved?"

"But I have studied all religions and have found that mine is the only true religion."

"But so have others studied other religions. What about them? Well I go further and tell you that religion is one and it has several branches which are all equal."

"I accept," said the professor, "that no religion lacks divine inspiration but all have not the same truth, because all have not the same light."

"It is an essentially untrue position to take, for a seeker after truth, that he alone is in absolute possession of truth.

What is happening to the poor astronomers today? They are changing their position every day, and there are scientists who impeach even Einstein's latest theory."

"No. But I have examined the arguments in favour of other religions."

"But it is an intellectual examination," said Gandhiji. "You require different scales to weigh spiritual truths. Either we are all untrue—quite a logical position to take,—but since truth does not come out of untruth it is better to say that we all have truth but not the complete truth. For God reveals His truth to instruments that are imperfect. Rain-drops of purest distilled water become diluted or polluted as soon as they come in contact with mother earth. My submission is that your position is arrogant. But I suggest to you a better position. Accept all religions as equal, for all have the same root and the same laws of growth."

But the good professor would still have his way and said, "It is necessary to examine every religion philosophically and find out which is more harmonious, more perfect."

"That presupposes that all religions are in watertight compartments. That is wrong. They are always growing," rejoined Gandhiji. "Let us not limit God's function. He may reveal Himself in a thousand ways and a thousand times."

Now the professor switched on to the next question, viz. that of fighting materialism.

"Well," said Gandhiji, "it is no use trying to fight these forces without giving up the idea of conversion, which I assure you is the deadliest poison that ever sapped the fountain of truth."

"But," said the professor, "I have a great respect for your religion."

"Not enough," said Gandhiji. "I had that feeling myself one day, but I found that it was not enough. Unless I accept the position that all religions are equal, and I have as much regard for other religions as I have for my own,

I would not be able to live in the boiling war around me. Any make-believe combination of spiritual forces is doomed to failure if this fundamental position is not accepted. I read and get all my inspiration from the Gita. But I also read the Bible and the Koran to enrich my own religion. I incorporate all that is good in other religions."

"That is your goodwill."

"That is not enough."

"But I have great respect for you."

"Not enough. If I were to join the Catholic Church, you would have greater respect for me?"

"Oh yes," said the professor with engaging naivete, "if you became a Catholic, you would be as great as St. Francis."

"But not otherwise? A Hindu cannot be a St. Francis? Poor Hindu!"

And there was loud laughter in which the professor joined.

*Harijan*, 16-1-'37 M. D.

## 7

## WITH AN AMERICAN CLERGYMAN

Dr. Crane, a distinguished clergyman from America was here the other day to visit Gandhiji. Born with a long military tradition behind him he had served in the last War, but left active service in the midst of it, as he could not stand the spectacle of a brother taking the life of a brother, and had since been hooted and mobbed as a pacifist. Dr. John Haynes Holmes' *New Wars for Old* had changed his outlook, and he had since consistently opposed war as a repudiation of Christianity. He was in Bombay on the Bakr-Id Day and had actually seen cows being slaughtered publicly. He had also been to a talkie—Tukaram—and had seen a crowded Hindu audience applaud miracles. He had travelled with a well-educated Hindu who had told him that he believed in miracles of that kind happening. He was puzzled and perplexed, probably because he did not distinguish between these outward forms of belief and the heart of the particular religions he had come across. At basis were not all the three religions one, and were not the representatives of each denying them at every step?

He wanted to understand Gandhiji's attitude towards Christianity, as he had heard diverse representations made about it, and he also wanted a simple statement regarding Gandhiji's attitude to religion in general.

"I shall certainly give you my reaction to Christianity," said Gandhiji. "Even when I was 18 I came in touch with good Christians in London. Before that I had come in touch with what I used then to call 'beef and beer-bottle Christianity', for these were regarded as the indispensable criteria of a man becoming a Christian, with also a third thing, namely adoption of a European style of dress. Those Christians were parodying St. Paul's teaching—'Call thou nothing unclean.' I went to London, therefore, with that prejudice against Christianity. I came across good Christians there who placed the Bible in my hands. Then I met numerous Christians in South Africa, and I have since grown to this belief that Christianity is as good and as true a religion as my own. For a time I struggled with the question, 'Which was the true religion out of those I knew?' But ultimately I came to the deliberate conviction that there was no such thing as only one true religion and every other false. There is no religion that is absolutely perfect. All are equally imperfect or more or less perfect. Hence the conclusion that Christianity is as good and true as my own religion. But so also about Islam or Zoroastrianism or Judaism.

"I therefore do not take as literally true the text that Jesus is the only begotten son of God. God cannot be the exclusive Father and I cannot ascribe exclusive divinity to Jesus. He is as divine as Krishna or Rama or Mahomed or Zoroaster. Similarly I do not regard every word of the Bible as the inspired word of God, even as I do not regard every word of the Vedas or the Koran as inspired. The *sum total* of each of these books is certainly inspired, but I miss that inspiration in many of the things taken individually. The Bible is as much a book of religion with me as the Gita and the Koran."

[With this he pointed to the two or three editions of the Koran with also a copy of the Bible lying on a bamboo-shelf in front of him. He had read numerous commentaries on the Bible, but had not read many commentaries on the Koran, and that is why there were more than one edition now in front of him.]

"Therefore," said he, "I am not interested in weaning you from Christianity and making you a Hindu, and I would not relish your designs upon me, if you had any, to convert me to Christianity! I would also dispute your claim that Christianity is the *only* true religion. It is *also* a true religion, a noble religion, and along with other religions it has contributed to raise the moral height of mankind. But it has yet to make a greater contribution. After all what are 2,000 years in the life of a religion? Just now Christianity comes to yearning mankind in a tainted form. Fancy bishops supporting slaughter in the name of Christianity!"

"But," asked Dr. Crane, "when you say that all religions are true, what do you do when there are conflicting counsels?"

"I have no difficulty," said Gandhiji, "in hitting upon the truth, because I go by certain fundamental maxims. Truth is superior to everything, and I reject what conflicts with it. Similarly that which is in conflict with non-violence should be rejected. And on matters which can be reasoned out that which conflicts with Reason must also be rejected."

"In matters which can be reasoned out?"

"Yes, there are subjects where Reason cannot take us far and we have to accept things on faith. Faith then does not contradict Reason but transcends it. Faith is a kind of sixth sense which works in cases which are without the purview of Reason. Well then, given these three criteria, I can have no difficulty in examining all claims made on behalf of religion. Thus to believe that Jesus is the only begotten son of God is to me against Reason, for God can't marry and beget children. The word 'son' there can only be used in a figurative sense. In that sense everyone who stands in the position of Jesus is a begotten son of God. If a man is spiritually miles ahead of us, we may say that he is in a special sense the son of God, though we are all children of God. We repudiate the relationship in our lives, whereas his life is a witness to that relationship."

"Then you will recognize degrees of divinity. Would you not say that Jesus was the most divine?"

"No, for the simple reason that we have no data. Historically we have more data about Mahomed than anyone else because he was more recent in time. For Jesus there is less data and still less for Buddha, Rama and Krishna; and when we know so little about them, is it not preposterous to say that one of them was more divine than another? In fact even if there were a great deal of data available, no judge should shoulder the burden of sifting all the evidence, if only for this reason that it requires a highly spiritual person to gauge the degree of divinity of the subjects he examines. To say that Jesus was 99 per cent divine, and Mahomed 50 per cent, and Krishna 10 per cent, is to arrogate to oneself a function which really does not belong to man."

"But," said Dr. Crane, "let us take a debatable point. Supposing I was debating between whether violence is justified or not. Mahomedanism would say one thing, Christianity another."

"Then I must decide with the help of the tests I have suggested."

"But does not Mahomed prescribe the use of the sword in certain circumstances?"

"I suppose most Muslims will agree. But I read religion in a different way. Khansaheb Abdul Gaffar Khan derives his belief in non-violence from the Koran, and the Bishop of London derives his belief in violence from the Bible. I derive my belief in non-violence from the Gita, whereas there are others who read violence in it. But if the worst came to the worst and if I came to the conclusion that the Koran teaches violence, I would still reject violence, but I would not therefore say that the Bible is superior to the Koran or that Mahomed is inferior to Jesus. It is not my function to judge Mahomed and Jesus. It is enough that my non-violence is independent of the sanction of scriptures. But the fact remains that religious books have a hold upon mankind which other books have not. They have made a greater impression on me than Mark Twain or, to take a more appropriate instance, Emerson. Emerson was a thinker. Jesus and Mahomed were through and through men of action in a sense Emerson would never be. Their power was derived from their faith in God."

"I will take a concrete instance now to show what I mean," said Dr. Crane. "I was terribly shocked on Monday. I counted 37 cows slain on the streets by Muslims in the name of religion, and in offence to the Hindu sentiment. I asked the Hindu friend who travelled with me why the Muslims did so. He said it was part of their religion. 'Is it part of their spiritual growth?' I asked him. He said it was. I met a Mussalman who said, 'We both please God and ourselves.' Now here was a Mussalman revelling in a thing that outrages you and me too. Do you think all this is counter to the Koran?"

"I do indeed," said Gandhiji, and he referred Dr. Crane

to the article he had written only last week. "Just as many Hindu practices—e.g. untouchability—are no part of Hindu religion, I say that cow-slaughter is no part of Islam. But I do not wrestle with the Muslims who believe that it is part of Islam."

"What do you say to the attempts to convert?"

"I strongly resent these overtures to utterly ignorant men. I can perhaps understand overtures made to me, as indeed they are being made. For they can reason with me and I can reason with them. But I certainly resent the overtures made to Harijans. When a Christian preacher goes and says to a Harijan that Jesus was the only begotten Son of God, he will give him a blank stare. Then he holds out all kinds of inducements which debase Christianity."

"Would you say a Harijan is not capable of reason?"

"He is. For instance, if you try to take work out of him without payment, he will not give it. He also has a sense of ethical values. But when you ask him to understand theological beliefs and categories he will not understand anything. I could not do so even when I was 17 and had a fair share of education and training. The orthodox Hindus have so horribly neglected the Harijan that it is astonishing how he adheres to the Hindu faith. Now I say it is outrageous for others to shake his faith."

"What about a man who says he is commanded by God to do violence?"

"There you would not put another God before him. You need not disturb his religion, but you will disturb his reason."

"But take Hitler. He says he is carrying out God's behest in persecuting the Jews and killing his opponents."

"You will not pit one word of God against another word of God. But you will have to bear down his reason. For him you will have to produce a miracle which you will do when Christians will learn the art of dying without killing in defence of what they hold dearer than religion.

But we can go on arguing like this endlessly. And then I may tell you that you are talking against time." And with this Gandhiji looked at the watch.

"Just one question, then. Would you say then that your religion is a synthesis of all religions?"

"Yes, if you will. But I would call that synthesis Hinduism, and for you the synthesis will be Christianity. If I did not do so, you would always be patronizing me, as many Christians do now, saying, 'How nice it would be if Gandhi accepted Christianity,' and Muslims would be doing the same saying, 'How nice it would be if Gandhi accepted Islam!' That immediately puts a barrier between you and me. Do you see that?"

"I do. Just one last question. In your Hinduism do you basically include the caste system?"

"I do not. Hinduism does not believe in caste. I would obliterate it at once. But I believe in *varnadharma* which is the law of life. I believe that some people are born to teach and some to defend and some to engage in trade and agriculture and some to do manual labour, so much so that these occupations become hereditary. The law of *varna* is nothing but the law of conservation of energy. Why should my son not be a scavenger if I am one?"

"Indeed? Do you go so far?"

"I do, because I hold a scavenger's profession in no way inferior to a clergyman's."

"I grant that, but should Lincoln have been a woodchopper rather than President of the U. S. A.?"

"But why should not a wood-chopper be a President of the United States? Gladstone used to chop wood."

"But he did not accept it as his calling."

"He would not have been worse off if he had done so. What I mean is, one born a scavenger must earn his livelihood by being a scavenger, and then do whatever else he likes. For a scavenger is as worthy of his hire as a lawyer or your President. That, according to me, is Hinduism. There is no better communism on earth, and I have illustrated it with one verse from the Upanishads which means: God pervades all—animate and inanimate. Therefore renounce all and dedicate it to God and then live. The right of living is thus derived from renunciation. It does not say, 'When all do their part of the work I too will do it.' It says, 'Don't bother about others, do your job first and leave the rest to Him.' *Varnadharma* acts even as the law of gravitation. I cannot cancel it or its working by trying to jump higher and higher day by day till gravitation ceases to work. That effort will be vain. So is the effort to jump over one another. The law of *varna* is the antithesis of competition which kills."

"I was simply thrilled, and am going away with much inspiration," said Dr. Crane to me as we returned to Wardha.

"That's because you are a pacifist," I said half seriously and half in joke. "A hostile attitude is the opposite of pacifism."

"I had not realized it," said Dr. Crane. "But you are right, peace has more implications than we know. If I had gone to argue I should have come away without taking anything; but I did not go to argue, I went to discuss."

But the Bakr-Id scene was haunting him. "Now please explain this thing to me if you can. What would Mr. Gandhi do if he was to witness such a scene?"

"He would stand between the slaughterer and the cow. He does not do so now, as we have not done enough to rise to that pitch of ultimate sacrifice."

"But he attaches the same value to the life of a cow as to the life of a human being?"

"He does. That is what Hinduism teaches us."

"But will these slaughters ever cease? Will anyone stand between the cow and the slaughterer?"

"Why not? You know something about Gandhiji's fasts? You know how Telemachus stopped the savage gladiatorial blood-sports in Rome, after they had lasted for seven centuries? But let that be. Do you know that in the year of grace 1921 there were practically no cow-sacrifices, for Mussalman leaders and divines appealed to the Muslim populace to have no such sacrifices?"

"Indeed? Why was that?"

"Then Hindus and Mussalmans were one. A great wave of unity had swept over the land."

"Why can't it do so today?"

"It can. Let us come to our own. There is a third power between us today which claims to maintain peace between us. Let it disappear and we will establish peace."

"That is what I am told will not happen."

"The proof of the pudding is in the eating. How can I prove it by argument?"

*Harijan,* 6-3-'37 M. D.

8

## COLOMBO Y. M. C. A.

Addressing a huge gathering in the hall of Y. M. C. A., Colombo, Gandhiji welcomed the occasion as one more instance of the close touch, he was daily finding himself in, of Christians throughout the world. 'There are some who will not even take my flat denial when I tell them that I am not a Christian,' said Gandhiji, and in trying to explain his own attitude to Christianity, gave in his own humble way a message to the whole of the Christian world.

*True Proselytization*

"The message of Jesus, as I understand it, is contained in his Sermon on the Mount unadulterated and taken as a whole, and even in connection with the Sermon on the Mount, my own humble interpretation of the message is in many respects different from the orthodox. The message, to my mind, has suffered distortion in the West. It may be presumptuous for me to say so, but as a devotee of truth, I should not hesitate to say what I feel. I know that the world is not waiting to know my opinion on Christianity.

"One's own religion is after all a matter between oneself and one's Maker and no one else's, but if I feel impelled to share my thoughts with you this evening, it is because I want to enlist your sympathy in my search for truth and because so many Christian friends are interested in my thoughts on the teachings of Jesus. If then I had to face only the Sermon on the Mount and my own interpretation of it, I should not hesitate to say, 'Oh yes, I am a Christian.' But I know that at the present moment if I said any such thing I would lay myself open to the gravest misinterpretation. I should lay myself open to fraudulent claims because I would have then to tell you what my own meaning of Christianity is, and I have no desire myself to give you my own view of Christianity. But negatively I can tell you that, in my humble opinion, much of what passes as Christianity is a negation of the Sermon on the Mount. And please mark my words. I am not at the present moment speaking of the Christian conduct. I am speaking of the Christian belief, of Christianity as it is understood in the West. I am painfully aware of the fact that conduct everywhere falls short of belief. But I don't say this by way of criticism. I know from the treasures of my own experience that, although I am every moment of my life trying to live up to my professions, my conduct falls short of these professions. Far, therefore, be it from me to say this in a spirit of criticism. But I am placing before you my fundamental difficulties. When I began as a prayerful student to study the Christian literature in South Africa in 1893, I asked myself 'Is this Christianity'? and have always got the Vedic answer, 'Neti, Neti' (not this, not this), and the deepest in me tells me that I am right.

"I claim to be a man of faith and prayer, and even if I was cut to pieces, God would give me the strength not to deny Him and to assert that He is. The Muslim says: He is and there is no one else. The Christian says the same thing and so the Hindu, and, if I may say so, even the Buddhist says the same thing, if in different words. We may each of us be putting our own interpretation on the word God,—God who embraces not only this tiny globe of ours, but millions and billions of such globes. How can we, little crawling creatures, so utterly helpless as He has made us, how could we possibly measure His greatness, His boundless love, His infinite compassion, such that He allows man insolently to deny Him, wrangle about Him, and cut the throat of his fellow-man? How can we measure the greatness of God who is so forgiving, so divine? Thus though we may utter the same words they have not the same meaning for us all. And hence I say that we do not need to proselytize or do Shuddhi or Tabligh through our speech or writing. We can only do it really with our lives. Let them be open books for all to study. Would that I could persuade the missionary friends to take this view of their mission. Then there will be no distrust, no suspicion, no jealousy and no dissensions."

*A Lesson from China*

Gandhiji then took the case of modern China as a case in point. His heart, he said, went out to Young China in the throes of a great national upheaval, and he referred to the anti-Christian movement in China, about which he had occasion to read in a pamphlet received by him from the students' department of the Young Women's Christian Association and Young Men's Christian Association of China. The writers had put their own interpretation upon the anti-Christian movement, but there was no doubt that Young China regarded Christian movements as being opposed to Chinese self-expression. To Gandhiji the moral of this anti-Christian manifestation was clear. He said: "Don't let your Christian propaganda be anti-national, say these young Chinese. And even their Christian friends have come to distrust the Christian endeavour that had come from the West. I present the thought to you that these essays written by young men have a deep meaning, a deep truth, because they were themselves trying to justify their Christian conduct in so far as they had been able to live up to the life it had taught them and at the same time find a basis for that opposition. The deduction I would like you all to draw from this manifestation is that you Ceylonese should not be torn from your moorings, and those from the West should not consciously or unconsciously lay violent hands upon the manners, customs and habits of the Ceylonese in so far as they are not repugnant to fundamental ethics and morality. Confuse not Jesus' teaching with what passes as modern civilization, and pray do not do unconscious violence to the people among whom you cast your lot. It is no part of that call, I assure you, to tear the lives of the people of the East by its roots. Tolerate whatever is good in them and do not hastily, with your preconceived notions, judge them. Do not judge lest you be judged yourselves. In spite of your belief in the greatness of Western civilization and in spite of your pride in all your achievements, I plead with you for humility, and ask you to leave some little room for doubt in which, as Tennyson sang, there was more truth, though by 'doubt' he no doubt meant a different thing. Let us each one live our life, and if ours is the right life, where is the cause for hurry? It will react of itself."

### *To the Young Ceylonese*

The Y. M. C. A. has among its members Buddhists also, and the president had specially asked Gandhiji to say a word of advice to the Christian and Buddhist youth. He gave them the following message:

"To you, young Ceylonese friends, I say: Don't be

dazzled by the splendour that comes to you from the West. Do not be thrown off your feet by this passing show. The Enlightened One has told you in never-to-be-forgotten words that this little span of life is but a passing shadow, a fleeting thing, and if you realize the nothingness of all that appears before your eyes, the nothingness of this material case that we see before us ever changing, then indeed there are treasures for you up above, and there is peace for you down here, peace which passeth all understanding, and happiness to which we are utter strangers. It requires an amazing faith, a divine faith and surrender of all that we see before us. What did Buddha do, and Christ do, and also Mahomed? Theirs were lives of self-sacrifice and renunciation. Buddha renounced every worldly happiness, because he wanted to share with the whole world his happiness which was to be had by men who sacrificed and suffered in search for truth. If it was a good thing to scale the heights of Mt. Everest, sacrificing precious lives in order to be able to go there and make some slight observations, if it was a glorious thing to give up life after life in planting a flag in the uttermost extremities of the earth, how much more glorious would it be to give not one life, surrender not a million lives but a billion lives in search of the potent and imperishbale truth! So be not lifted off your feet, do not be drawn away from the simplicity of your ancestors. A time is coming when those, who are in the mad rush today of multiplying their wants, vainly thinking that they add to the real substance, real knowledge of the world, will retrace their steps and say, 'What have we done?' Civilizations have come and gone, and in spite of all our vaunted progress I am tempted to ask again and again, 'To what purpose?' Wallace, a contemporary of Darwin, has said the same thing. Fifty years of brilliant inventions and discoveries, he has said, has not added one inch to the moral height of mankind. So said a dreamer and visionary if you will—Tolstoy. So said Jesus, and Buddha, and Mahomed, whose religion is being denied and falsified in my own country today.

"By all means drink deep of the fountains that are given to you in the Sermon on the Mount, but then you will have to take sackcloth and ashes. The teaching of the Sermon was meant for each and every one of us. You cannot serve both God and Mammon. God the Compassionate and the Merciful, Tolerance incarnate, allows Mammon to have his nine days' wonder. But I say to you, youths of Ceylon, fly from that self-destroying but destructive show of Mammon."

*God's Temples*

Here in Ceylon where I am writing for *Young India* amid surroundings where Nature has bountifully poured her richest treasure, I recall a letter written by a poetically inclined friend from similar scenes. I share with the reader a paragraph from that letter:

> "A lovely morning! Cool and cloudy, with a drowsy sun whose rays are as soft as velvet. It is a strangely quiet morning—there is a hush upon it, as of prayer. And the mists are like incense, and the trees worshippers in a trance, and the birds and insects pilgrims come to chant *bhajans*. Oh! how I wish one could learn true abandonment from Nature! We seem to have forgotten our birthright to worship where and when and how we please. We build temples and mosques and churches to keep our worship safe from prying eyes and away from outside influences, but we forget that walls have eyes and ears, and the roofs might be swarming with ghosts—who knows?
>
> Good Gracious, I shall find myself preaching next! How foolish on a lovely morning like this! A little child in the garden adjoining is singing as unconsciously and joyously as a bird. I feel inclined to go and take the dust of its little feet. And since I cannot pour out my heart in sound as simply as that little one, my only refuge is in silence!"

Churches, mosques and temples, which cover so much hypocrisy and humbug and shut the poorest out of them, seem but a mockery of God and His worship, when one sees the eternally renewed temple of worship under the vast blue canopy inviting every one of us to real worship, instead of abusing His name by quarrelling in the name of religion.

*Young India*, 8-12-'27 M. D.

## 9

## THINGS OF THE SPIRIT

I propose to put together here some of the things I could not include in my weekly letters. It is generally known now that Christian missionaries everywhere seek Gandhiji out to have a talk with him on things of the spirit. But very rarely does one raise a question—as Mr. De Boer at Vellore did—as to what exactly Gandhiji means by 'things of the spirit', and why. Sometimes one gets an impression as though they delighted in riddling him with questions like those that a Protestant might put to a Jesuit or *vice versa*, and as a result they get more confounded than ever. I cannot express my feeling in the matter better than a European lady did at the end of the Conference with the missionaries in Colombo. 'I wanted,' she said, 'to ask Gandhiji about the spiritual meaning of Khadi, and what he expects us Westerners to do in that behalf. Instead these friends asked questions which were hardly of immediate concern.' All friends are aware by now that only one mission and one alone takes Gandhiji from one end of the country to the other, and one would feel thankful if they took a leaf out of this lady's book.

But to turn to some of the questions. Just as a Protestant would ask a Jesuit as to what he meant by the doctrine of obedience, a friend at the Colombo meeting asked what Gandhiji thought of the possibility of the forgiveness of sin. Gandhiji explained at length how there could be no forgiveness like the forgiveness that a criminal prays for and gets from an earthly king. It was a question of a change of heart brought about by true contrition, a ceaseless striving for purification. In this connection Gandhiji referred to the case of the Plymouth Brother whom he has himself made historic by a detailed reference in the Autobiography. "But the Plymouth Brother I met," said Gandhiji, "argued that there was no such thing as human effort. If you accept the fact of crucifixion, sinfulness would go altogether. I was astounded as I knew and was intimate with quite a number of Christian friends who were making a definite effort. 'Don't you fall?' I asked him. 'Yes,' he said, 'but my strength comes from the fact that Jesus intercedes for me and washes my sins away.' Well, I tell you the Quaker friend who had introduced me to the Plymouth Brother felt no less astounded. Asking for forgiveness means that we should not sin again, and the grant of forgiveness means that we would have power to resist all temptation. It is only after a persistent, untiring effort that God comes to our rescue as a wall of protection and there is a growing consciousness that we shall not sin. In a famous controversy with Huxley, I remember Gladstone having said that when the definite grace of God was pledged to us we became incapable of sin. Jesus was incapable of sin from birth, Gladstone said, but we could be such by constant striving. So long as there is a single evil thought coming to our mind, we must conclude that there is not complete forgiveness or grace."

Another friend wondered if Gandhiji's position in matters of faith was not like living in a sort of half-way house.

"I certainly admire the friend who made that criticism," said Gandhiji, "but he may be sure that there is no half-way house for me. I have been described as an intolerable wholehogger. I know that friends get confused when I say I am a Sanatanist Hindu and they fail to find in me things they associate with a man usually labelled as such.

But that is because in spite of my being a staunch Hindu I find room in my faith for Christian and Islamic and Zoroastrian teaching, and therefore my Hinduism *seems* to some to be a conglomeration and some have even dubbed me as an eclectic. Well, to call a man eclectic is to say that he has no faith, but mine is a broad faith which does not oppose Christians, not even a Plymouth Brother, not even the most fanatical Mussalman. It is a faith based on the broadest possible toleration. I refuse to abuse a man for his fanatical deeds, because I try to see them from his point of view. It is that broad faith that sustains me. It is a somewhat embarrassing position, I know, but to others, not to me!"

At another meeting of the missionaries (at Jaffna) he developed this last thought, in reply to a question as to what he would wish India to be like in matters of religion. He reiterated his impatience with the missionary or the Mussalman who thinks of getting hold of the 'untouchable' for the sake of increasing his flock, and said that like the Dewan of Mysore he would ask them all to strive to make the 'untouchables' better Hindus if they could. "I should love," he said, "all the men, not only in India but in the world, belonging to the different faiths, to become better people by contact with one another and, if that happens, the world will be a much better place to live in than it is today. I plead for the broadest toleration, and I am working to that end. I ask people to examine every religion from the point of the religionists themselves. I do not expect the India of my dream to develop one religion, i.e., to be wholly Hindu, or wholly Christian, or wholly Mussalman, but I want it to be wholly tolerant, with its religions working side by side with one another."

One of the missionary friends wanted to know how the Gita and the New Testament compared as sources of comfort so far as Gandhiji was concerned, and instead of giving a bald answer that he derived all the comfort that he needed from the Bhagavadgita, he retold the story of the beginnings of his religious studies in England, with which the readers of the Autobiography are in the main familiar. All missionaries seem to forget that the men they approach with their gospel have their traditions and their own religion which sustain them from generation to generation. Gandhiji told these friends that when he read the Sermon on the Mount he read nothing new, but found in it, vividly told, what he had learnt in his childhood. 'There is nothing much in giving a cup of water to one who gave you a cup of water, or saluting one who salutes you, but there is some virtue in doing a good turn to one who has done you a bad turn.' "I have not been able to see," he said, "any difference between the Sermon on the Mount and the Bhagavadgita. What the Sermon describes in a graphic manner, the Bhagavadgita reduces to a scientific formula. It may not be a scientific book in the accepted sense of the term, but it has argued out the law of love—the law of abandon as I would call it—in a scientific manner. The Sermon on the Mount gives the same law in wonderful language. The New Testament gave me comfort and boundless joy, as it came after the repulsion that parts of the Old had given me. Today supposing I was deprived of the Gita and forgot all its contents but had a copy of the Sermon, I should derive the same joy from it as I do from the Gita."

And as though summing up the argument with a great warning, he said, "*You know there is one thing in me, and that is that I love to see the bright side of things and not the seamy side,* and so I can derive comfort and inspiration from any great book of any great religion. I may not be able to reproduce a single verse from the Gita or the New Testament, a Hindu child or Christian child may be able to repeat the verses better, but those clever children cannot deprive me of the assimilation that is in me today of the spirit of the two books."

*Young India*, 22-12-'27 M. D.

# 10

# INTERNATIONAL FELLOWSHIP CONVENTION

## *Friends of a Feather*

Two events of a far-reaching importance occurred last week—the visit to the Ashram of friends of the International Fellowship, and the Convocation of the Vidyapith. And if I devote more space to the one than to the other, it is not because I attach more value to it, but because it is not so familiar as the other coming every year.

It was in the fitness of things that the members of the Council of the International Federation with their friends should have thought of having their meeting in the Ashram, itself an international fellowship in its own way. If the friendly company that visited us was as varied as it could be, no less varied were we their hosts — men and women drawn from different countries and bound together by a common ideal. It is possible that the friends came to Sabarmati attracted by the name of the Ashram and its founder, but I have no doubt that many of them left with the feeling that during the three days that they spent with us they were amidst another fellowship inspired as much as they by the ideal of peace on earth and goodwill to men.

To take only a few names, among our guests were friends like Deenabandhu Andrews, the warmth of whose friendship and co-operation any association working for peace must prize; friends like Professor P. A. Wadia, a Zoroastrian, loving 'to scorn delight and live laborious days', like Mr. De Boer from Vellore and Mr. Dewick from the other end of India, Calcutta, and Mr. and Mrs. Henriod from Switzerland, working for the welfare of the student world; ladies like Miss Varley from Madras, loving to call herself 'a mother of three hundred children', and Shrimati Janaki Ammal from Malabar and Mrs. Maclean and

Miss Manibai from Bombay and Miss Van Doren from Poona, all fired with the same ideals of social service; men like Mr. Elwin of the Society of Christ, just out of his teens and fresh from Oxford, come to India, as he said, to do some atonement for the sin of his countrymen in keeping India in chains; Indian friends like Dr. Jesudasan and Sjt Sankaran Nair and Mr. Hameed Khan from South India and Mr. Kumaraswamy from Ceylon—Christians, Hindus, a Parsi and a Moslem; Indians, Americans, English, Swiss, a Russian and a Swede—a fellowship of faiths and nationalities and aspirations for goodwill and unity. They have an Indian secretary in Mr. A. A. Paul, loved by them all, and ever active and industrious.

They stayed with us for three days and came in fairly close contact with the members of our Ashram, rejoicing to conform to all our rules of daily life and contenting themselves with the meagre comforts that it was in our power to give them. Many of them took part in the morning prayer and all in the evening prayer, English translations of our verses and songs being specially supplied to them, and in addition to the Indian songs usually sung we had a hymn each day given us by the Christian congregation. We were thus a happy fraternity enjoying these days of privilege and grace.

*The Foundation of Fellowship*

Prof. Wadia opened the sessions with a devotional speech of which the keynote was love, not only between individuals and individuals, but nations and nations. The next day Mr. Andrews led with readings from the Bible and 'When I survey the wondrous Cross', and invited Khare Shastri to give a song from the Ashram Bhajanavali and Imamsaheb to recite verses from the Holy Koran. After this Gandhiji was requested to open a discussion on what should be the fundamental objective of the fellowship. There was no doubt about their object, but they had yet to formulate a creed which whilst it was free from narrowness was also free from any trace of latitudinarianism. The discussion lasted for two days, and though they could not arrive at any definite result, it was far from fruitless. It led to a free and frank exchange of views ultimately bound to establish a better understanding. It also showed that, however much we swear by the fundamentals, most of us labour under what Bacon classified as the idols of the tribe, the cave, the forum and the theatre. Thus there was no difference of opinion as to the object of all to work for the widest toleration, to combine and side with the forces of light against the forces of darkness or, as Deenabandhu Andrews said, with those who seek God, truth and divine light, against those who blankly leave God out and become materialists. Everyone seemed to be agreed on this, but many seemed to run away from what would appear to be the necessary corollary of the proposition. This was defined by Gandhiji at some length at this and other meetings, and the discussion clearly showed the various points of contact and difference.

"In order to attain a perfect fellowship," said Gandhiji, "every act of its members must be a religious act and an act of sacrifice. I came to the conclusion long ago, after prayerful search and study and discussion with as many people as I could meet, that all religions were true and also that all had some error in them, and that whilst I hold by my own, I should hold others as dear as Hinduism, from which it logically follows that we should hold all as dear as our nearest kith and kin and that we should make no distinction between them. So we can only pray, if we are Hindus, not that a Christian should become a Hindu, or if we are Mussalmans, not that a Hindu or a Christian should become a Mussalman, nor should we even secretly pray that any one should be converted, but our inmost prayer should be that a Hindu should be a better Hindu, a Muslim a better Muslim and a Christian a better Christian. That is the fundamental truth of fellowship. That is the meaning of the wonderful passion, the story of which Andrews read out to you, of the song and verses that Khare Shastri and Imamsaheb recited. If Andrews invited them to give their song and verses for mere courtesy or by way of patronizing toleration, he was false to the fellowship. In that case he should not have done so. But I have known Charlie Andrews too well, and I know that he has given the same love to others as he has for his own, and thereby broadened his Christianity, as I broaden my Hinduism by loving other religions as my own. If, however, there is any suspicion in your minds that only one religion can be true and others false, you must reject the doctrine of fellowship placed before you. Then we would have a continuous process of exclusion and found our fellowship on an exclusive basis. Above all I plead for utter truthfulness. If we do not feel for other religions as we feel for our own, we had better disband ourselves, for we do not want a wishy-washy toleration. My doctrine of toleration does not include toleration of evil, though it does the toleration of the evil-minded. It does not therefore mean that you have to invite each and every one who is evil-minded or tolerate a false faith. By a true faith I mean one the sum total of whose energy is for the good of its adherents; by a false I mean that which is predominantly false. If you, therefore, feel that the sum total of Hinduism has been bad for the Hindus and the world, you must reject it as a false faith."

*Conversion*

Gandhiji's insistence on a member of the fellowship not even secretly wishing that a member of another faith should be converted to his own, led to a general discussion on the question of conversion. Gandhiji again defined his position more clearly than before: "I would not only not try to convert but would not even secretly pray that anyone should embrace my faith. My prayer would always be that Imamsaheb should be a better Mussalman, or become the best he can. Hinduism with its message of *ahimsa* is to me the most glorious religion in the world,—as my wife to me is the most beautiful woman in the world,—but others may feel the same about their own religion. Cases of real honest conversion are quite possible. If some people for their inward satisfaction and growth change their religion, let them do so. As regards taking our message to the aborigines, I do not think I should go and give my message out of my own wisdom. Do it in all humility, it is said. Well, I have been an unfortunate witness of arrogance often going in the garb of humility. If I am perfect, I know that my thought will reach others. It taxes all my time to reach the goal I have set to myself. What have I to take to the aborigines and the Assamese hillmen except to go in my nakedness to them? Rather than ask them to join my prayer, I would join their prayer. We were strangers to this sort of classification—'animists', 'aborigines', etc., but we have learnt it from the English rulers. I must have the desire to serve and it must put me right with people. Conversion and service go ill together."

The next day early morning the friends met for an informal conversation with Gandhiji when again the same question was asked by many of them.

'Would you have a ruling of such a character that those who had a desire to convert should not be eligible for membership?'

'Personally,' said Gandhiji, 'I think they should not be eligible. I should have framed a resolution to that effect as I regard it as the logical outcome of fellowship. It is essential for inter-religious relationship and contact.'

'Is not the impulse to proselytize God-given?' inquired another friend.

'I question it,' said Gandhiji. 'But if all impulses are God-given, as some of our Hindus believe, He has also given us discrimination. He will say, I have given you many impulses so that your capacity to face temptation may be tested.

'But you do believe in preaching an economic order?' inquired one of the fair sex.

'I do, as I believe in preaching laws of health.'

'Then why not apply the same rule in religious matters?'

'It is a relevant question. But you must not forget that we have started with the fundamental principle that all religions are true. If there were different but good and true health laws for different communities, I should hesitate to preach some as true and some as false. I am positive that with people not prepared to tolerate one another's religious belief there can be no international fellowship.'

'Moreover physical analogies when applied to spiritual matters are good only up to a certain point. When you take up an analogy from nature you can stretch it only to a certain point. But I would take an illustration from the physical world and explain what I mean. If I want to hand a rose to you, there is a definite movement. But if I want to transmit its scent, I do so without any movement. The rose transmits its own scent without a movement. Let us rise a step higher, and we can understand that spiritual experiences are self-acting. Therefore the analogy of preaching sanitation etc. does not hold good. If we have spiritual truth, it will transmit itself. You talk of the joy of a spiritual experience and say you cannot but share it. Well, if it is real joy, boundless joy, it will spread itself without the vehicle of speech. In spiritual matters we have merely to step out of the way. Let God work His way. If we interfere we may do harm. Good is a self-acting force. Evil is not, because it is a negative force. It requires the cloak of virtue before it can march forward.'

'Did not Jesus himself teach and preach?'

'We are on dangerous ground here. You ask me to give my interpretation of the life of Christ. Well, I may say that I do not accept everything in the gospels as historical truth. And it must be remembered that he was working amongst his own people, and he said he had not come to destroy but to fulfil. I draw a great distinction between the Sermon on the Mount and the Letters of Paul. They are a graft on Christ's teaching, his own gloss apart from Christ's own experience.'

*Young India*, **19-1-'28** **M. D.**

## 11

## A WORD TO THE MISSIONARIES

The progress of the anti-untouchability campaign is being watched carefully and critically, and servants in the cause cannot be too mindful of the self-purification aspect of the movement. It is said to have disturbed some of our Missionary friends. Gandhiji has had letters from some of them, and a friend, discussing the matter with Gandhiji the other day, summed it up this way: "Your campaign is taking away from the Missionary's popularity."

"I see what you mean," said Gandhiji, "but I do not know why it should disturb them. We are not traders trenching on one another's province. If it is a matter of serving oneself, I should understand their attitude, but when it is entirely a matter of serving others, it should not worry them or me as to who serves them."

"But, perhaps, the authorities in charge of a Mission hospital would rightly feel worried, if you sent your people to go and open a hospital in the same place."

"But they should understand that ours is a different mission. We do not go there to afford them simply medical relief or a knowledge of the three R's; our going to them is a small proof of our repentance and our assurance to them that we will not exploit them any more. I should never think of opening a hospital where there is already one; but if there is a Mission school, I should not mind opening another for Harijan children, and I would even encourage them to prefer our school to the other. Let us frankly understand the position. If the object is purely humanitarian, purely that of carrying education where there is none, they should be thankful that someone whose obvious duty it is to put his own house in order wakes up to a sense of his duty. But my trouble is that the Missionary friends do not bring to bear on their work a purely humanitarian spirit. Their object is to add more members to their fold, and that is why they are disturbed. The complaint which I have been making all these years is more than justified by what you say. Some of the friends of a Mission were the other day in high glee over the conversion to Christianity of a learned pandit. They have been dear friends, and so I told them that it was hardly proper to go into ecstasies over a man forsaking his religion. Today it is the case of a learned Hindu, tomorrow it may be that of an ignorant villager not knowing the principles of his religion. Why should Missionaries complain, if I open a school which is more liked by Harijans than theirs? Is it not natural?"

"But does it mean that you would say the same thing about a Christian who embraces Hinduism?"

"I would. Here is Mirabehn. I would have her find all the spiritual comfort she needs from Christianity, and I should not dream of converting her to Hinduism, even if she wanted to do so. Today it is the case of a grown-up woman like her, tomorrow it may be that of a European child trusted to my care by a friend. Take the case of Khan Saheb's daughter entrusted to my care by her father. I should jealously educate her in her own faith and should strive my utmost against her being lured away from it, if ever she was so inclined. I have had the privilege of having children and grown-up persons of other faiths with me. I was thankful to find them better Christians, Mussalmans, Parsis or Jews by their contact with me."

"But if it was a pure case of conscience?"

"I am no keeper of anybody's conscience, but I do feel that it argues some sort of weakness on the part of a person who easily declares his or her failure to derive comfort in the faith in which he or she is born."

Evidently there is a fundamental difference between the two viewpoints. But let Missionary friends remember that it was none but that most Christ-like of all Christians, Albert Schweitzer, who gave Christianity a unique interpretation when he himself resolved "not to preach any more, not to lecture any more", but to bury himself in Equatorial Africa simply with a view to fulfil somewhat the debt that Europe owes to Africa.

*Harijan*, 25-1-'35 M. D.

## 12

## A RUDE SHOCK

A Polish research student stayed away to be introduced to Gandhiji after the students of the Institute had left, having had a chat with Gandhiji and his blessings to be torch-bearers of truth and worthy successors of Sir Chandrasekhara. He said he did not want any talk with Gandhiji. I took him in and let him sit before Gandhiji for a second. But as he was getting up he pulled out from his pocket a photograph on which he wanted Gandhiji's autograph. "Why?" asked Gandhiji. He answered: "I am keenly interested in rural reconstruction. There is at...a school conducted by Catholic Fathers. I shall help the school from the proceeds of the sale of this photograph." "Ah," said Gandhiji, returning the photograph, "that is a different story. You do not expect me to support the Fathers in their mission of conversion? You know what they do?"

And with this he told him in a couple of minutes the story of the so-called conversions in the vicinity of Tiruchengodu, the desecration and demolition of the Hindu temple, how he had been requested by the International Fellowship of Faiths to forbear writing anything about the episode as they were trying to intervene, how ultimately even the intervention of that body composed mainly of Christians had failed, and how he was permitted to write about it in *Harijan*. He, however, had deliberately refrained from writing, in order not to exacerbate feelings on the matter.

"But," said the student, "the Christians among whom the Fathers I mention are working became Christians long ago."

"Well, there they foment fresh troubles. I do not know why the professors of a noble faith should assist in creating deadly quarrels between two sections of the same faith."

"But I myself am a Christian convert. I cannot tell you the happiness and the solace that Christianity has meant to me."

"I can understand that. You are using the language of a truly converted Christian. You have a heart to lose or to keep. If the Harijans in India reach your intellectual and spiritual level, and experience your sense of original sin, I would bless them for voluntarily embracing Christianity. Have you read what I have written on my son's so-called conversion to Islam? If he had become a Muslim from a pure and a contrite heart, I should have no quarrel with him. But those who had helped him to embrace Islam and are enthusing over his apostacy simply exploited his weaknesses. They are no true representatives of Islam. My letter to the Muslims, I tell you, was written with my pen dipped in my heart's blood. Similarly there is no redeeming feature about the Tiruchengodu conversions I have spoken to you about."

The young man could see the deep pain with which Gandhiji was speaking. He did not press him to give the autograph and took his leave.

*Harijan*, 27-6-'36 M. D.

## 13

## A DISCOURSE WITH CHRISTIAN FRIENDS

Dr. Ceresole walked one morning to Sevagram, wading through ankle-deep mud and had long talks with Gandhiji in his hut. He is a pilgrim to the Kingdom of Heaven, and he loves to compare notes when he meets a kindred spirit like Gandhiji.

"Religion," he said, "which should bind us divides us. Is it not a sorry spectacle that, whilst people of various denominations find no difficulty in working together all day in hearty co-operation, they must disband when the time for prayer comes? Is religion then meant to divide us? Must it be allowed to become an expression of conceit rather than of a desire to be of service?"

Dr. Ceresole thus did some loud thinking when he went to Sevagram one morning with two missionary ladies. "I want," he said, "some sort of religious communion between men of different faiths."

"Quite possible," said Gandhiji, "if there is no mental reservation."

"But a friend of mine, a great humanitarian worker," said Dr. Ceresole, "believes that but for evangelism he should not have taken up his mission work. He gets the driving power from communion with Jesus, he says, because Jesus was always in communion with God."

"The greatest trouble with us is," said Gandhiji, "not that a Christian missionary should rely on his own experience, but that he should dispute the evidence of a Hindu devotee's life. Just as he has his spiritual experience and the joy of communion, even so has a Hindu."

Dr. Ceresole seemed to have no doubt about this, and he said that the broadest view of Christianity seemed to him to have been presented by Frank Lenwood whose book *Jesus—Lord or Leader* deserved to be better known than it is. "He says he has the greatest respect for the personality of Jesus, but he thought he might respectfully criticize him."

But the mention of mental reservation led the missionary visitors to raise the question of questions, so far as missionaries in India are concerned. "I have not had the time or desire to evangelize," one of them said. "The Church at home would be happy if through our hospital more people would be led to Christian lives."

"But whilst you give the medical help you expect the reward in the shape of your patients becoming Christians."

"Yes, the reward is expected. Otherwise there are many other places in the world which need our service. But instead of going there, we come here."

"There is the kink. At the back of your mind there is not pure service for its sake, but the result of service in the shape of many people coming to the Christian fold."

"In my own work there is no ulterior motive. I care for people, I alleviate pain, because I cannot do otherwise. The source of this is my loyalty to Jesus who ministered to suffering humanity. At the back of my mind there is, I admit, the desire that people may find the same joy in Jesus that I find. Where is the kink?"

"The kink is in the Church thinking that there are people in whom certain things are lacking, and that you must supply them whether they want them or not. If you simply say to your patients, 'You have taken the medicine I gave you. Thank God. He has healed you. Don't come again,' you have done your duty. But if you also say, 'How nice it would be if you had the same faith in Christianity as I have,' you do not make of your medicine a free gift."

"But if I feel that I have something medically and spiritually which I can give, how can I keep it?"

"There is a way out of the difficulty. You must feel that what you possess, your patient also can possess but through a different route. You will say to yourself, 'I have come through this route, you may come through a different route.' Why should you want him to pass through your University and no other?"

"Because I have my partiality for my Alma Mater."

"There is my difficulty. Because you adore your mother, you cannot wish that all the rest were your mother's children."

"That is a physical impossibility."

"Then this one is a spiritual impossibility. God has the whole humanity as his children. How can I limit God's grace by my little mind and say this is the only way?"

"I do not say it is the only way. There might be a better way."

"If you concede that there might be a better way, you have surrendered your point."

"Well if you say that you have found your way, I am not so terrifically concerned with you. I will deal with one who is floundering in mud."

"Will you judge him? Have you people not floundered? Why will you present your particular brand of truth to all?"

"I must present to them the medicine I know."

"Then you will say to him, 'Have you seen your own doctor?' You will send him to his doctor, and ask the doctor to take charge of him. You will perhaps consult that doctor, you will discuss with him the diagnosis, and will convince him or allow yourself to be convinced by him. But there you are dealing with a wretched physical thing. Here we are dealing with a spiritual thing where you cannot go through all these necessary investigations. What I plead for is humanity. You do not claim freedom from hypocrisy for the Christian Church?"

Dr. Ceresole: "Most of us believe our religion to be the best, and they have not the slightest idea of what other religions have revealed to their adherents. Dr.—has made a careful study of the Hindu scriptures, and he has observed what Hinduism gives to the Hindus."

"I say it is not enough for him to read the Song Celestial or the Koran. It is necessary for him to read the Koran with Islamic spectacles and the Gita with Hindu spectacles, just as he would expect me to read the Bible with Christian spectacles. I would ask him: 'Have you read the Gita as reverently as I have or even as reverently as I have read the Bible?' I tell you I have not read as many books on Hinduism as I have about Christianity. And yet I did not come to the conclusion that Christianity or Hinduism was the *only* way."

Gandhiji discussed the instance of Mr. Stokes—now Shri Satyanand—who was in his early years in India nearly killed for preaching Christianity to the Pathans, but who in a truly Christian spirit secured his assailant's reprieve, and who in the later years said to himself, "My faith in Jesus is as bright as ever, but I cannot deliver the message of Jesus to the Hindus unless I become a Hindu." "Unless I make the Hndus better Hindus I shall not," he said, "be true to my Lord."

But, then, wondered the missionary friends, what exactly should be the missionaries' attitude?

"I think," said Gandhiji, "I have made it clear. But I shall say it again in other words: *Just to forget that you have come to a country of heathens, and to think that they are as much in search of God as you are; just to feel that you are not going there to give your spiritual goods to them, but that you will share your worldly goods of which you have a good stock. You will then do your work without a mental reservation and thereby you will share your spiritual treasures.* The knowledge that you have this reservation creates a barrier between you and me."

"Do you think that, because of what you call that mental reservation, the work that one could accomplish would suffer?"

"I am sure. You would not be half as useful as you would be without the reservation. The reservation means that you belong to a different and a higher species, and you make yourself inaccessible to others."

"A barrier would be certainly my Western way of living."

"No, that can be immediately broken."

"Would you be really happy if we stayed at home?"

"I cannot say that. But I will certainly say that I have never been able to understand your going out of America. Is there nothing to do there?"

"Even in America there is enough scope for educational work."

"That is a fatal confession. You are not a superfluity there. But for the curious position that your Church has taken, you would not be here."

"I have come because the Indian women need medical care to a greater extent than American women do. But coupled with that I have a desire to share my Christian heritage."

"That is exactly the position I have been trying to counter. You have already said that there may be a better way."

"No, I meant to say that there may be a better way fifty years hence."

"Well we were talking of the present, and you said there might be a better way."

"No, there is no better way today than the one I am following."

"That is what I say is assuming too much. You have not examined all religious beliefs. But even if you had, you may not claim infallibility. You assume knowledge of all people, which you can do only if you were God. I want you to understand that you are labouring under a double fallacy: That what you think is best for you is really so; and that what you regard as the best for you is the best for the whole world. It is an assumption of omniscience and infallibility. I plead for a little humility."

*Harijan*, 18-7-'36 M. D.

## 14

## EQUALITY OF RELIGIONS

As one reads Mrs. Polak's book, *Mr. Gandhi the Man*, giving intimate glimpses of Gandhiji's ever-growing family in South Africa more than 25 years ago, one finds that he is living here the same life, making the same experiments, trying to water the same roots of human brotherhood. In South Africa too there were Mussalmans and Christians in the household, and not only all followed their own religious practices but each co-operated with the other heartily in seeing that the practices were observed without a hitch or a jar. When the days of Ramzan came and the Mussalman members fasted without having even a drop of water during long hours, the Hindu members vied with one another in preparing all kinds of delicacies for those who had to break their fast after sunset, and the children, I suppose, looked forward to the break of the fast as they had a share of the nice things.

Thanks to the presence of Khansaheb Abdul Gaffar Khan with his daughter at Sevagram, those days are being repeated here on a very small scale. There was perhaps a little more indulgence in South Africa in the matter of food, and the Khansaheb is certainly not like the Mussalman friends in South Africa who loved the good things of life. He begins his day with his early prayers at four o'clock and a light repast of milk and fruit before dawn. The prayers in South Africa were perhaps not so systematic as they have become during recent years, and a special feature of the prayers these days is that the Khansaheb leads with a text from the Koran which he explains in the briefest sentence or two, and then follow the Sanskrit verses.

The presence of the Khansaheb in Sevagram is important for several reasons. He shares with interest some of the deepest talks on religion that take place nowadays and often makes important contributions, as he did when Deenabandhu Andrews was in Sevagram for some mornings during the last week. I shall reserve Gandhiji's talks with Dr. John Mott for a future letter, contenting myself with giving the salient features of the talks with the Deenabandhu.

He had just returned from a visit to New Zealand, Fiji and Australia where he had numerous talks about the situation in India and about the work of the various Missionary Societies in India. He had, since his arrival in India, been in correspondence with various Missionaries and wanted to know from Gandhiji his reaction to the present attitude of the Missionaries. "Their behaviour," said Gandhiji, "has been as bad as that of the rest who are in the field to add to their numbers. What pains one is their frantic attempt to exploit the weakness of Harijans. If they said, 'Hinduism is a diabolical religion and you come to us,' I should understand. But they dangle earthly paradises in front of them and make promises to them which they can never keep. When in Bangalore a deputation of Indian Christians came to me with a number of resolutions which they thought would please me, I said to them: 'This is no matter for bargain. You must say definitely that this is a matter to be settled by the Hindus themselves. Where is the sense of talking of a sudden awakening of spiritual hunger among the 'untouchables' and then trying to exploit a particular situation? The poor Harijans have no mind, no intelligence, no sense of difference between God and no-God. It is absurd for a single individual to talk of taking all the Harijans with himself. Are they all bricks that they can be moved from one structure to another? If Christian Missions here want to play the game, and for that matter Mussalmans and others, they should have no such idea as that of adding to their ranks whilst a great reform in Hinduism is going on."

C. F. A.: "Let me ask one question. I said in Australia that all the talk of Dr. Ambedkar and his followers was not in terms of religion, and I said also that it was cruelty to bargain with unsophisticated people like the Harijans as they are in most parts of India. Then came the London Missionary Society's statement that the Ezhavas in Travancore had asked for Christian instruction. I said then that the Ezhavas were quite enlightened and, if they had really asked to be instructed in Christianity, it would be an entirely different matter. Was I right?"

Gandhiji: "I do not think so. Whilst there are individual Ezhavas who are doctors and barristers and so on, the vast majority of them are just the same as the Harijans elsewhere. I can assure you that no one representing the vast body of Ezhavas could have asked for Christian instruction. You should ascertain the fact from our principal workers there."

C. F. A.: "I see what you mean. Only I wanted to say that the London Missionary Society was a liberal body and would not make an irresponsible statement."

Gandhiji: "But they at the centre cannot know, as the Parliament cannot know the truth of what is happening in India."

C. F. A.: "But that apart, I should like to discuss the fundamental position with you. What would you say to a man who after considerable thought and prayer said that he could not have his peace and salvation except by becoming a Christian?"

Gandhiji: "I would say that, if a non-Christian (say a Hindu) came to a Christian and made that statement, he should ask him to become a good Hindu rather than find goodness in change of faith."

C. F. A.: "I cannot in this go the whole length with you, though you know my own position. I discarded the position that there is no salvation except through Christ long ago. But supposing the Oxford Group Movement people changed the life of your son, and he felt like being converted, what would you say?"

Gandhiji: "I would say that the Oxford Group may change the lives of as many as they like, but not their religion. They can draw their attention to the best in their respective religions and change their lives by asking them to live according to them. There came to me a man, the son of Brahman parents, who said his reading of your book had led him to embrace Christianity. I asked him if he thought that the religion of his forefathers was wrong. He said 'No.' Then I said: 'Is there any difficulty about your accepting the Bible as one of the great religious books of the world and Christ as one of the great teachers?' I said to him that you had never through your books asked Indians to take up the Bible and embrace Christianity, and that he had misread your book—unless of course your position is like that of the late Maulana Mahomed Ali's, viz. that a believing Mussalman, however bad his life, is better than a good Hindu."

C. F. A.: "I do not accept M. Mahomed Ali's position at all. But I do say that, if a person really needs a change of faith, I should not stand in his way."

Gandhiji: "But don't you see that you do not even give him a chance? You do not even cross-examine him. Supposing a Christian came to me and said he was captivated by a reading of the Bhagavat and so wanted to declare himself a Hindu, I should say to him: 'No. What the Bhagavat offers the Bible also offers. You have not yet made the attempt to find it out. Make the attempt and be a good Christian.' "

C. F. A.: "I don't know. If someone earnestly says that he will become a good Christian, I should say, 'You may become one,' though you know that I have in my own life strongly dissuaded ardent enthusiasts who came to me. I said to them, 'Certainly not on *my* account will you do anything of the kind.' But human nature does require a concrete faith."

Gandhiji: "If a person wants to believe in the Bible, let him say so, but why should he disregard his own religion? This proselytization will mean no peace in the world. Religion is a very personal matter. We should by living the life according to our lights share the best with one another, thus adding to the sum total of human effort to reach God."

"Consider," continued Gandhiji, "whether you are going to accept the position of mutual toleration or of equality of all religions. My position is that all the great religions are fundamentally equal. We must have the innate respect for other religions as we have for our own. Mind you, not mutual toleration, but equal respect."

C. F. A.: "What do you say, Khansaheb, to all this?"

Khansaheb: "Take it from me that the world is never going to have *one* religion. All religions are equal, all prophets are equal. A true Mussalman, to my mind, is one who carries out the will of Allah. I do not know how M. Mahomed Ali came to take up the position he did. I cannot at all accept it. I can never accept a wicked Mussalman as a Mussalman at all, and not worth comparing with Father Elwin or Mahatmaji. The pity is we do not know religion, and if we know the principles, we have no grip on them. All religions are springs running from the same source, and nourish different soils and different people. Why should a Mussalman go crazy over making other people Mussalmans, and a Christian over making other people Christians? After all, in spite of all our proselytizing zeal, where are we? What progress have we made?"

*Harijan*, 28-11-'36 M. D.

## 15

## MISSIONARY METHODS

The question of missionary methods has been discussed threadbare in these columns, and friends interesting themselves in them should by now know well enough Gandhiji's attitude to them. But they all broach the question nevertheless, and as Gandhiji's views have never the defect of staleness, I must set out here Gandhiji's replies to Mr. Basil Mathews' questions at some length. Mr. Mathews referred to the Archbishop of Canterbury's speech at the Central Hall, Westminster. "That is a question to which I have given great thought," said Gandhiji, "and I am convinced that, if Christian Missions will sincerely play the game, no matter what may be their policy under normal circumstances, they must withdraw from the indecent competition to convert the Harijans. Whatever the Archbishop of Canterbury and others may say, what is done here in India in the name of Christianity is wholly different from what they say. There are others in the field also, but as a devotee of truth I say that, if there is any difference between their methods, it is one of degree and not of kind. I know of representatives of different religions standing on the same platform and vying with one another to catch the Harijan ear. To dignify this movement with the name of spiritual hunger is a travesty of truth. Arguing on the highest plane I said to Dr. Mott, if they wanted to convert Harijans, had they not better begin to convert me? I am a trifle more intelligent than they, and therefore more receptive to the influences of reason that could be brought to bear upon me. But to approach the Pulayas and Pariahs with their palsied hands and paralysed intelligence is no Christianity. No, whilst our reform movement is going on, all religious-minded people should say: Rather than obstruct their work, let us support them in their work."

Mr. Mathews: Do not the roots of the reform movement go back to the missionary movement? Did not the missionaries wake up the reformers and make a certain amount of stir among the untouchables?

Gandhiji: I do not think that the missionary movement was responsible for a stirring of the right kind. I agree that it stung the reformers to the quick and awakened them to their sense of duty. They say: 'Here is some good work being done by these missionaries; they open schools and hospitals, train nurses. Why don't we do these things for our own people?' And they try to do something in indifferent imitation.

Mr. M: You have spoken of some good work being done by missionaries. Should not we go on with it?

G: Oh yes. Do, by all means. But give up what makes you objects of suspicion and demoralizes us also. We go to your hospitals with the mercenary motive of having an operation performed, but with no object of responding to what is at the back of your mind, even as our children do when they go to Bible classes in their colleges and then laugh at what they read there. I tell you our conversation at home about these missionary colleges is not at all edifying. Why then spoil your good work with other motives?

The scope of *Harijan* precludes me from including here questions that touched on politics.

Mr. Mathews was curious to know if Gandhiji followed any spiritual practices and what special reading he had found helpful.

Gandhiji: I am a stranger to *yogic* practices. The practice I follow is a practice I learnt in my childhood from my nurse. I was afraid of ghosts. She used to say to me: 'There are no ghosts but if you are afraid, repeat *Ramanama*.' What I learnt in my childhood has become a huge thing in my mental firmament. It is a sun that has brightened my darkest hour. A Christian may find the same solace from the repetition of the name of Jesus, and a Muslim from the name of Allah. All these things have the same implications and they produce identical results under identical circumstances. Only the repetition must not be a lip expression, but part of your very being. About helpful readings, we have regular readings of the Bhagavadgita and we have now reached a stage when we finish the Gita every week by having readings of appointed chapters every morning. Then we have hymns from the various saints of India, and we therein include hymns from the Christian hymn book. As Khansaheb is with us, we have readings from the Koran also. We believe in the equality of all religions. I derive the greatest consolation from my reading of Tulsidas's Ramayana. I have also derived solace from the New Testament and the Koran. I don't approach them with a critical mind. They are to me as important as the Bhagavadgita, though everything in the former may not appeal to me—everything in the Epistles of Paul, for instance—nor everything in Tulsidas. The Gita is a pure religious discourse given without any embellishment. It simply describes the progress of the pilgrim soul towards the Supreme Goal. Therefore there is no question of selection.

Mr. Mathews: You are really a Protestant.

G.: I do not know what I am or am not. Mr. Hodge will call me a Presbyterian!

*Q*. Where do you find the seat of authority?

*A*. It lies here (pointing to his breast). I exercise my judgment about every scripture, including the Gita. I cannot let a scriptural text supersede my reason. Whilst I believe that the principal books are inspired, they suffer from a process of double distillation. Firstly they come through a human prophet, and then through the commentaries of interpreters. Nothing in them comes from God directly. Mathew may give one version of one text and John may give another. I cannot surrender my reason whilst I subscribe to divine revelation. And above all, 'the letter killeth, the spirit giveth life.' But you must not misunderstand my position. I believe in faith also, in things where reason has no place, e.g. the existence of God. No argument can move me from that faith, and like that little girl who repeated against all reason 'yet we are seven' I would like to repeat, on being baffled in argument by a very superior intellect, 'Yet there is God.'

*Harijan*, 5-12-'36 M. D.

16

## TRUE EVANGELISM

There were visitors during the week interested in Christian mass movements, and they came with a number of questions which seem to be agitating all thinking missionaries. They were greatly in earnest and their questions were well thought-out.

*Q*. Do you see a reason for Christian workers in the West to come here, and if so what is their contribution?

*A*. In the manner in which they are working, there would seem to be no room for them. Quite unconsciously they do harm to themselves and so to us. It is perhaps impertinent for me to say that they do harm to themselves, but quite pertinent to say that they do harm to us. They do harm to those amongst whom they work and those amongst whom they do not work, i.e. the harm is done to the whole of India. They present a Christianity of their belief but not the message of Jesus as I understand it. The more I study their activities the more sorry I become. There is such a gross misunderstanding of religion on the part of those who are intelligent, very far advanced, and whose motives need not be questioned. It is a tragedy that such a thing should happen in the human family.

*Q*. You are referring to things as they are at present. Do you visualize a situation in which there is a different approach?

*A*. Your ability is unquestioned. You can utilize all those abilities for the service of India which she would appreciate. That can only happen if there are no mental reservations. If you come to give education, you must give it after the Indian pattern. You should sympathetically study our institutions and suggest changes. But you come with preconceived notions and seek to destroy. If people from the West came on Indian terms, they would supply a felt want. When Americans come and ask me what service they can render, I tell them: 'If you dangle your millions before us, you will make beggars of us and demoralize us.' But in one thing I do not mind being a beggar. I would beg of you your scientific talent. You can ask your engineers and agricultural experts to place their services at our disposal. They must not come to us as our lords and masters but as volunteer workers. A paid servant would throw up his job any day, but a volunteer worker could not do so. If such come, the more the merrier. A Mysore engineer (who is a Pole) has sent me a box of hand-made tools made to suit village requirements. Supposing an engineer of that character comes and studies our tools and our cottage machines and suggests improvements in them, he would be of great service. If you do this kind of work in a religious spirit, you will have delivered the message of Jesus.

*Q*. There is this mood abroad in the world.

*A*. I would like to see it amongst missionaries in general in India.

*Q*. What would happen if there is an increase in the process of multiplying Christians?

*A*. If there is an appreciable increase, there would be blood feuds between Harijans themselves, more savage than the feuds we have in Bombay. 50 per cent of the residents in Sevagram are Harijans. Supposing you stole away 10 Harijans and built a church for them, you would set up father against son and son against father, and you would find texts in the Bible to support your action. That would be a caricature of Christianity.

Here Gandhiji explained that the whole story of the sudden uprush of spiritual hunger among the millions of untouchables was absurd. A speech at Central Hall, Westminster, made by Bishop Pickett, of which he had read a report in *The Church Times* had greatly shocked him. "He has," he said, "made such extravagant statements that I would want a demonstration of them—even of the statement that millions were *seeking* to be converted."

*Q*. Apart from the contribution through the realm of scientific achievement, evangelism seems to you to be out of the question in establishing relationships between East and West.

*A*. I do say that. But I speak with a mental reservation. I cannot only reconcile myself to—I must recognize—a fact in nature which it is useless to gainsay—I mean proper evangelization. When you feel you have received peace from your particular interpretation of the Bible, you share it with others. But you do not need to give vocal expression to it. Your whole life is more eloquent than your lips. Language is always an obstacle to the full expression of thought. How, for instance, will you tell a man to read the Bible as *you* read it, how by word of mouth will you transfer to him the light as you receive it from day to day and moment to moment? Therefore all religions say: 'Your life is your speech.' If you are humble enough, you will say you cannot adequately represent your religion by speech or pen.

*Q.* But may not one in all humility say, 'I know that my life falls far short of the ideal, let me explain the ideal I stand for'?

*A.* No. You bid good-bye to humility the moment you say that life is not adequate and that you must supplement it by speech. Human species need not go to animals and shout to them: 'We are humans.' The animals know them as humans. The language of the soul never lends itself to expression. It rises superior to the body. Language is a limitation of the truth which can be only represented by life.

*Q.* How then is experience to be passed on from generation to generation without some articulate expression?

*A.* There is no occasion for articulate expression. Life is its own expression. I take the simile of the rose I used years ago. The rose does not need to write a book or deliver a sermon on the scent it sheds all around, or on the beauty which everyone who has eyes can see. Well, spiritual life is infinitely superior to the beautiful and fragrant rose, and I make bold to say that the moment there is a spiritual expression in life, the surroundings will readily respond. There are passages in the Bible, the Gita, the Bhagawat, the Koran, which eloquently show this. "Wherever," we read, "Krishna appeared, people acted like those possessed." The same thing about Jesus. But to come nearer home, why are people touched as if by magic wherever Jawaharlal goes? They sometimes do not even know he has come, and yet they take sudden fire from the very thought that he is coming. Now there it may not be described as a spiritual influence, but there is a subtle influence and it is unquestionably there, call it by what name you like. They do not want to hear him, they simply want to see him. And that is natural. You cannot deal with millions in any other way. Spiritual life has greater potency than Marconi waves. When there is no medium between me and my Lord and I simply become a willing vessel for His influences to flow into it, then I overflow as the water of the Ganges at its source. There is no desire to speak when one lives the truth. Truth is most economical of words. There is thus no truer or other evangelism than life.

*Q.* But if a person were to ask the source of such a life, what then?

*A.* Then you will speak, but your language will be well thought-out. You will yourself feel that. It defies expression. But then the questioner probes further, if he is a searcher. Then you will draw him to you. You will not need to go to him. Your fame will so spread that people from all parts of the world will flock to see you and listen to you. You will then speak to them. Take Aurobindo Ghose. Many from all parts go to him. He does not even see them, except on two days during the year, and never talks to them.

*Q.* Do you see any indication that there is a drawing together of those who have intimations of a higher life?

*A.* Yes. But not through these organizations. They are a bar to the process. Why am I at Sevagram? Because I believe that my message will have a better chance of penetrating the masses of India, and may be through them to the world. I am otherwise not a man capable of shutting myself up. But I am so down-right natural that once I feel a call I go forward with it, whatever happens. Mr. Hofmeyr of the South African Delegation appreciated my desire not to move out, he did not resent it as pride or indifference. Economy of words and action has, therefore, its value. Only it has to be natural.

*Harijan*, 12-12-'36 M. D.

17

## THE KOTTAYAM INTERVIEW

[On the 19th January last Gandhiji had a private talk with Bishop Moore of Travancore and Bishop Abraham of Mar Thoma and other friends at Kottayam. I found a wholly inaccurate account of this in *The Madras Mail*, and at Gandhiji's instance sent to the gentleman responsible for it a correct version according to us. He was good enough to accept it and had it approved by the Bishops. Here is the agreed version, with a slight alteration by Bishop Moore incorporated in it.—M. D.]

Advantage was taken of Gandhiji's visit to Kottayam for an interview between him and Christian friends there at the suggestion of a common friend. The interview took place at the Bishop's house, in the afternoon of 19th January. Bishop Moore, Bishop Abraham, Mr. Kuruvilla, and several other friends were present.

The object of the interview was to clear up the misunderstandings that had been created over Gandhiji's writings in *Harijan* in respect of Bishop Pickett's speech at a missionary meeting in London and a widely distributed C. M. S. appeal for funds.

Bishop Moore received Gandhiji cordially and welcomed the Temple Entry Proclamation as an important event. He inquired if the Savarnas and Brahmins also welcomed it, or if there was any opposition on their part.

Gandhiji said he had seen no signs of opposition. He had met several thousands of people, visited several temples, and had found Savarnas and Avarnas entering the temples in perfect friendliness.

Bishop Abraham asked if the Ezhavas were ready to treat the depressed classes of lower castes on terms of equality.

Gandhiji said he could not reply with confidence but he was striving to emphasize that point everywhere, and he hoped that the Proclamation would be carried out in that spirit.

Bishop Moore now came to the main subject of the talk of that afternoon. He said that he had heard that Mr. Gandhi was disturbed over reports of Christian missionary work in Travancore, and that he was ready to remove any misunderstanding that it was possible for him to remove.

Gandhiji said that he was indeed surprised at the report of conversions of thousands of people in the Telugu country and in Travancore made in Bishop Pickett's speech in England and in a statement of the Church Missionary Society appealing for funds over the signature of Prebendary Cash. He could not understand how responsible Christians could make extravagant statements to the effect that thousands had experienced a spiritual awakening and accepted the Gospel. The Bishop of Dornakal had even stated that these thousands included not only the Depressed Classes but a large number of so-called high caste Hindus. Gandhiji said he had challenged the truth of these statements in the columns of *Harijan* and had invited those concerned to prove that he was wrong. He had also met leaders working in Andhra and asked them to make inquiries into the truth of these extravagant statements.

Bishop Moore confessed that he had not read either the appeal for funds or Bishop Pickett's speech, and could not, therefore, express any opinion thereon. He was quite sure, however, that no responsible missionary journal should ever publish statements that were not based on actual facts, and he wanted to assure Mr. Gandhi that no wrong information had ever been supplied from his diocese for which alone he could speak. He could, of course, say nothing about the Bishop of Dornakal's diocese, except that the Bishop when he was on a visit to Travancore had made definite statements to that effect. So far as Travancore was concerned he supposed that Mr. Gandhi was aware that quite independently of Dr. Ambedkar's appeal there was a stir among the Ezhavas, a large number of whom expressed a desire to embrace Christianity. This movement was strong from last February to May, but since then had considerably weakened. At no time could the Bishop say that in his diocese the Ezhavas had come in their thousands to ask for baptism, and during the last year they could record 530 persons as having been baptized into the Anglican faith. During the above movement among the Ezhavas the Bishop felt that it was only proper for them to respond to the demand for spiritual instruction, but they had always made it a point not to admit anyone to membership of the Church without being fully satisfied that after due instruction the persons concerned had realized to the full all the spiritual implications of a change of faith.

Bishop Abraham said he had been to the Andhra country and had seen with his own eyes that there was a tremendous awakening there even among the middle class Savarnas. He could not say that any one of them had accepted Christ, but he had addressed meetings which were attended by many of the high caste people.

"But that," said Gandhiji, "means nothing. Hundreds of students attend meetings addressed by Dr. Stanley Jones, but they cannot be said to seek conversion to Christianity. To say that hundreds attended meetings addressed by Christian preachers is very different from saying that hundreds have accepted the message of Jesus, and from making an appeal for money in anticipation of people becoming Christians in large numbers."

Bishop Abraham said the practice in his own diocese was as Bishop Moore had described. He gave the instance of a man who saw him at a late hour of the night wanting to be baptized there and then. He advised him to wait, but he came again and said that if he was not accepted he would have to approach some other Church. He was ultimately admitted into the Mar Thoma Church after the Bishop was thoroughly satisfied about his faith in Jesus.

Mr. Kuruvilla here put in whether Mr. Gandhi had any objection to their stimulating and responding to the spiritual hunger of people.

Gandhiji said it was wholly irrelevant to the issue.

Bishop Abraham said as Mr. Kuruvilla had rightly put it, they were responding to the spiritual hunger of the people. Mr. Gandhi could have no objection to that?

Gandhiji said he could have no objection to responding to spiritual hunger, provided it was genuinely felt and expressed. But the matter was quite irrelevant to the discussion which was entirely about extravagant statements made by responsible people. He said to Bishop Moore that he would furnish him with a copy of the C. M. S. statement, and he would like to know what Bishop Moore would have to say regarding it.

Bishop Moore said it was no use troubling Mr. Gandhi for the statement which he felt sure that he could procure for himself. He was sorry that he had not yet read it, but he said he would do so now and send his opinion to Mr. Gandhi.

*Harijan*, 13-3-'37

## 18

# WITH AN INDIAN MISSIONARY

*Right and Duty*

An Indian Christian Missionary had a long talk with Gandhiji the other day during which he put to Gandhiji questions arising from Gandhiji's recent criticism of a joint manifesto issued by several influential Indian Christians. It will be remembered that Gandhiji in his article commented at length particularly on the portion of the manifesto wherein the manifesto made this claim on behalf of the Christian Church: "The Church will cling to its right to receive such people into itself from whatever religious group they may come. It will cling to the further right to go about in these days of irreligion and materialism to awaken spiritual hunger in all."

"I have been following," said the visitor, "your comments on the statements regarding mass movements made by the Indian Christians. I wonder if those who made the statement were thinking of anything in the nature of a *legal* right. It is, I think, a moral right they claim here rather than a legal one."

"My criticism would apply even if they had used the word 'moral right'. But it is clear that they mean a legal right, because for one thing there is no such thing as a moral right, and secondly because in the very next para of the manifesto, in which they have referred to the Karachi Resolution on Fundamental Rights, they make it clear that they mean by 'right' legal right. A moral right, if there is any such thing, does not need any asserting and defending."

"The main purpose of the manifesto was to check the agitation that is going on in certain quarters. I admit that, if it was meant to be a protest, it was not properly drafted."

"That is why," said Gandhiji, "I have called it 'an unfortunate document'. And is there anything like a moral right? Give me an illustration."

"Have I not a moral right to speak?"

"It is not a moral right but a legal right. There is no right but is legal. Divorced from legality a moral right is a misnomer. And therefore you either enforce a right or fight for it. Whereas nobody asserts one's duty. He humbly performs it. I shall take an illustration. You are here. You feel like preaching to me the Gospel. I deny the right and ask you to go away. If you regard praying for me a duty, you will quietly go away and pray for me. But if you claim the right to preach to me, you will call the police and appeal to them for preventing my obstructing you. That leads to a clash. But your duty no one dare question. You perform it here or elsewhere, and if your prayers to God to change my heart are genuine, God will change my heart. What Christianity, according to my interpretation of it, expects you to do is to pray to God to change my heart Duty is a debt. Right belongs to a creditor, and it would be a funny thing indeed if a devout Christian claimed to be a creditor!"

*Spread Your Perfume*

"You have objected to Christian propaganda on the ground that Harijans are illiterate and ignorant. What would you say of propaganda amongst non-Harijans?"

"I have the same objection, because the vast mass of people of India would not understand the pros and cons of Christianity better than a cow. I repeat this simile in spite of the fact that it has been objected to. When I say I do not understand logarithms any better than my cow, I do not mean any insult to my intelligence. In matters of theology the non-Harijan masses can understand no better than Harijans. I would take you to Sevagram and show you that there is no distinction so far as capacity to understand such things is concerned, between Harijans and non-Harijans. Try to preach the principles of Christianity to my wife. She can understand them no better than my cow. I can, because of the training that I have had."

"But," objected the friend, "we do not preach any theology. We simply talk of the life of Christ and tell them what a comfort his life and teaching have been to us. He has been our guide, we say, and ask others also to accept Him as their guide."

"Oh yes, you do say that. But when you say I must accept Jesus in preference to Ramakrishna Paramahamsa, you will have to go into deep waters. That is why I say, let your life speak to us, even as the rose needs no speech but simply spreads its perfume. Even the blind who do not see the rose perceive its fragrance. That is the secret of the gospel of the rose. But the gospel that Jesus preached is more subtle and fragrant than the gospel of the rose. If the rose needs no agent much less does the gospel of Christ need any agent."

*The Mental Reservation*

"But then your objection is to the commercial aspect of the Christian propaganda. Every true Christian will agree that no baits should be offered."

"But what else is Christianity as it is preached nowadays? Not unless you isolate the proselytizing aspect from your educational and medical institutions are they any worth. Why should students attending Mission schools and colleges be compelled or even expected to attend Bible classes? If they must understand the message of Jesus, why not also of Buddha, Zoroaster and Mahomed? Why should the bait of education be offered for giving education?"

"That was the old way, not the modern way."

"I can cite to you any number of modern examples. Is not the Bishop of Dornakal a modern? And what else is his Open Letter to the Depressed Classes of India? It is full of baits."

"He represents a type of Christianity which I do not approve. But where there is no compulsion to attend the Bible classes and only education is given, what objection is there to educational institutions run by Missions?"

"There is a subtle kind of propaganda when you expect students to attend Bible classes."

"As regards hospitals, I think philanthropy without the dynamic of some religious teaching will not tell."

"Then you commercialize your gift, for at the back of your mind is the feeling that because of your service some day the recipient of the gift will accept Christ. Why should not your service be its own reward?"

"But leave alone these. I think I can cite instances of exceptionally fine people who attract people to them by the example of their lives."

"I too can cite such instances. Andrews is one such. But they are exceptions."

"But then you must judge Christianity by its best representatives, and not the worst."

"I am not judging Christianity as a religion. I am talking of the way Christianity is being propagated, and you cannot judge it by exceptions, even as you may not judge the British system of government by some fine specimens of Englishmen. No, let us think of the bulk of your people who preach the Gospel. Do they spread the perfume of their lives? That is to me the sole criterion. All I want them to do is to live Christian lives, not to annotate them. I have come to this view after laborious and prayerful search, and I am glad to say that there is a growing body of Christians who accept my view."

*Personality of Jesus*

"Then, I should be obliged to hear from you your attitude to the personality of Jesus."

"I have often made it clear. I regard Jesus as a great teacher of humanity, but I do not regard him as the only begotten son of God. That epithet in its material interpretation is quite unacceptable. Metaphorically we are all begotten sons of God, but for each of us there may be different begotten sons of God in a special sense. Thus for me Chaitanya may be the only begotten son of God."

"But don't you believe in the *perfection* of human nature, and don't you believe that Jesus had attained perfection?"

"I believe in the *perfectibility* of human nature. Jesus came as near to perfection as possible. To say that he was perfect is to deny God's superiority to man. And then in this matter I have a theory of my own. Being necessarily limited by the bonds of flesh, we can attain perfection only after dissolution of the body. Therefore God alone is absolutely perfect. When He descends to earth, He of His own accord limits Himself. Jesus died on the Cross because he was limited by the flesh. I do not need either the prophecies or the miracles to establish Jesus' greatness as a teacher. Nothing can be more miraculous than the three years of his ministry. There is no miracle in the story of the multitude being fed on a handful of loaves. A magician can create that illusion. But woe worth the day on which a magician would be hailed as the saviour of humanity. As for Jesus raising the dead to life, well I doubt if the men he raised were really dead. I raised a relative's child from supposed death to life, but that was because the child was not dead, and but for my presence there she might have been cremated. But I saw that life was not extinct. I gave her an enema and she was restored to life. There was no miracle about it. I do not deny that Jesus had certain psychic powers and he was undoubtedly filled with the love of humanity. But he brought to life not people who were dead but who were believed to be dead. The laws of Nature are changeless, unchangeable, and there are no miracles in the sense of infringement or interruption of Nature's laws. But we limited beings fancy all kinds of things and impute our limitations to God. We may copy God, but not He us. We may not divide Time for Him, Time for Him is eternity. For us there is past, present and future. And what is human life of a hundred years but less than a mere speck in the eternity of Time?"

*Harijan*, 17-4-'37 M. D.

## 19

## THE MOST EFFECTIVE WAY

A missionary friend who was on a visit to us asked Gandhiji what was the most effective way of preaching the gospel of Christ, for that was his mission. This was Gandhiji's reply:

"To live the gospel is the most effective way—most effective in the beginning, in the middle and in the end. Preaching jars on me and makes no appeal to me, and I get suspicious of missionaries who preach. But I love those who never preach but live the life according to their lights. Their lives are silent, yet most effective, testimonies. Therefore I cannot say what to preach, but I can say that a life of service and uttermost simplicity is the best preaching. If, therefore, you go on serving people and ask them also to serve, they would understand. But you quote instead John 3,16 and ask them to believe it. That has no appeal to me, and I am sure people will not understand it. Where there has been acceptance of the gospel through preaching, my complaint is that there has been some motive."

"But we also see it," said the friend," and we try our best to guard against it."

"But you can't guard against it. One sordid motive vitiates the whole preaching. It is like a drop of poison which fouls the whole food. Therefore I should do without any preaching at all. A rose does not need to preach. It simply spreads its fragrance. The fragrance is its own sermon. If it had human understanding and if it could engage a number of preachers, the preachers would not be able to sell more roses than the fragrance itself could do. The fragrance of religious and spiritual life is much finer and subtler than that of the rose."

But all this apparently failed to be of effect, and the reverend gentleman retired with an imprecation (or was it a blessing?): "Mr. Gandhi, you are getting old, and soon there will come a day when you will be judged, not in *your* righteousness, but in the righteousness of Jesus." He evidently did not know that any strength of right and purity that Gandhiji has, he attributes wholly and solely to God.

Another group of missionary friends came from Nagpur the other day—all ladies—with a number of questions. The first was whether, when we concentrated on the health and welfare of the villages, we were going in for medical relief to any extent.

"We are not going in for medical relief," said Gandhiji, "but for prevention. Therefore we concentrate on sanitation and hygiene. I am of opinion that a good deal of medical help is given only in order to make people more helpless. Medical help, in most cases, is practically thrown at them, and so it is lost on them. Some of my co-workers are going to a village close by where the streets are covered with filth. No wonder if the eyes of the children there are bad and there are all kinds of diseases. Just now our workers' efforts do not seem to make any impression on the villagers; but when they find that, as a result of their village having become cleaner and free from filth, they are also comparatively free from disease, they will appreciate the difference. Now, if you had a free dispensary there and were giving doses of medicine to all that came, you would make no headway. Tackling the village sanitation is the only really substantial work. There is an evil at our doors which is perfectly preventable and yet we have suffered our villagers to tolerate it for scores of years. It is an uphill task, whilst the distribution of free medicine is much easier. But I am asking my co-workers to avoid the easy thing and cheap applause. We must first concentrate on the prevention of disease, we can tackle the disease itself later on."

"Then you won't have doctors?"

"No, if you will not misunderstand me. I have done medical relief work myself. Only last month Harijans in Kathiawad were given free medical relief by doctors who performed operations for cataract and other diseases of the eyes. But I am just now talking of measures for the preservation of general health, and even when my workers have achieved the preliminary task of cleaning the villages, I should equip them with just four things—quinine, castor oil, bicarbonate of soda and iodine. No fifth thing is necessary."

"You seem to give the last place in your programme to schools?"

"No. We are conducting numerous schools for Harijans and giving numerous scholarships to Harijan boys. What is the use of my adding the school programme to the work of the Industries Association? It is intended to supplement the work of the Harijan Sangh and the Spinners' Association. This last has a capital of Rs. 20 lakhs to operate upon, and the Harijan Sangh has also a fair amount of funds. I must now launch a campaign, I said to myself, which needs very little funds and which adds to the pockets of the poor. Thus, if I could simply ask the villagers not to waste the human manure but to turn it to good account, I should, without any capital outlay, help them to save Rs. 50 crores every year. This turning of human evacuations to rich manure by superficial burial I learnt from Dr. Poore, and it is the simplest and the most effective method, whereas the activated sludge plan and the septic tank are comparatively expensive things."

The question of questions had been reserved until the last: "Does your Harijan Sangh do anything for the spiritual welfare of the people?"

"With me," said Gandhiji, "moral includes spiritual, and so my answer to your question will be 'everything' and 'nothing': 'Nothing', because we have no department to look after their spiritual welfare; 'Everything', because we expect the personal touch of the workers to transform the men among whom they are working. Even as it is, we are caught in the coil of hypocrisy; but when you set apart a department for the work, you make the thing doubly difficult. In my career as a reformer I have regarded everything from the moral standpoint. Whether I am engaged in tackling a political question or a social or economic one, the moral side of it always obtrudes itself and it pervades my whole attitude. But I admit I have no special department to look after the Harijans' spiritual welfare."

"But we, Christians, feel that we, who have something to share, must share it with others. If we want consolation, we find it from the Bible. Now, as for the Harijans, who have no solace to get from Hinduism, how are we to meet their spiritual needs?"

"By behaving just like the rose. Does the rose proclaim itself, or is it self-propagated? Has it an army of missionaries proclaiming its beauties?"

"But supposing some one asked us, 'Where did you get the scent?' "

"The rose, if it had sense and speech, would say, 'Fool, don't you see that I got it from my Maker?' "

"But if some one asks you, 'Then, is there no book?' "

"You will then say, 'Yes, for me there is the Bible.' If they were to ask me, I would present to some the Koran, to some the Gita, to some the Bible and to some Tulsidas'

Ramayana. I am like a wise doctor prescribing what is necessary for each patient."

"But I find difficulty in getting much from the Gita."

"You may, but I do not find any difficulty in getting much from the Bible as well as from the Koran."

*Harijan*, **29-3-'35** M. D.

20

## DR. MOTT'S VISIT

### I

*A Great Evangelist*

The reader will perhaps like to know something about Dr. John Mott before I proceed to summarize the two long and important conversations that he had with Gandhiji over a fortnight ago. One of the most energetic evangelists that ever lived, he has gone round the world several times taking the message of Christ to sixty-eight countries, and addressing millions of students in the world. Author of the World's Student Christian Federation, he is also the Chairman of the International Missionary Council and President of the World's Alliance of the Y. M. C. A. and has, during his active life of nearly fifty years—he is 71—, had intimate contacts with, as his biographer says, "men and women ranging from Mahatma Gandhi and Tolstoy to President Masaryk and Lord Grey, Andrew Carnegie and Kerensky and most of the rulers of the nations of his time". The significance of his life, according to Mr. Basil Mathews, the biographer, "seems to lie in the fact that he has dedicated and disciplined every power of body, mind and spirit to incessant battle across the world, through decade after decade, for the Kingdom of God."

How similar the object, to all seeming, to that to which Gandhiji has dedicated his life! And yet how different the moulds in which the two lives are cast! Dr. Mott has gone out to all parts of the earth as a crusader, Gandhiji has gone nowhere except where the work called him. Dr. Mott has dedicated himself to "incessant battle for the Kingdom of God", which according to him opens to those who receive Christ "as the only Saviour and Lord"; Gandhiji has sought to battle with the forces of darkness, with the weapons of Truth, Non-violence and Purity, the only symbols, according to him, of the Kingdom of God. For his work for the emancipation of the depressed and the downtrodden Gandhiji has collected millions, but he never swears by the power of money. Dr. Mott has collected very much more than Gandhiji and would collect still more, for he believes that money "is itself accumulated power. It is not only potent, but in some respects it is well-nigh omnipotent." "Here are 500 Bibles lying idle in a store room. Money puts them into circulation. One of them leads to the conversion of a man who in turn leads scores of other men to Christ," says Dr. Mott. "Money," he sums up, "is stored-up personality." Gandhiji would perhaps reverse the epigram and say: "Stored-up personality is money." Gandhiji believes in the equality of all religions, and has hence no religious mission, in the accepted sense of the word. Dr. Mott not only believes "in the adequacy of the Christian message for the world's need", but he feels that no other has that adequacy. He sees in Christ "the Desire of All Nations".

In a letter that Dr. Mott wrote in 1913 from a ship taking him to Rangoon, he deplored the fact that he "met Missionaries (in India) who after twenty-five years' labour had not seen an educated Indian baptized." He was encouraged to learn, however, "that before we sailed from India already six of the inquirers had been baptized." "Although the results of these meetings in India were as large proportionately as in Japan and China," he wrote in 1902, "it is not wise to give out the numbers in connection with evangelistic work in India and Ceylon until men have actually gone forward to baptism. To get men to make an open profession by baptism is far, far more difficult in India than in any other land where I have worked. To this end earnest efforts are being made to follow up these men."

A cursory reading of Mr. Basil Mathews' book *John R. Mott—World Citizen* has yielded to me these few basic facts of Dr. Mott's life, and it is well to remember these as a background to the conversation that took place. He had in mind what the Christians believe to be an unprecedented ferment among the 'untouchables' in India, and he came with a desire to help. "You have been one," said he to Gandhiji, "that has given a great initiative to the movement, you have put your life-blood into it, you have suffered and triumphed, and I want you to help me to a profound understanding of what the issues are and tell me how I may help, for I do not want to hinder. What is happening in India is going to have a profound effect on the world. We are in front of forces of which the influence it would be difficult to prophesy or predict. Give me your own diagnosis of the problem."

*A Problem of Life and Death*

Gandhiji: "So far as I am concerned with the untouchability question, it is one of life and death for Hinduism. As I have said repeatedly, if untouchability lives Hinduism perishes, and even India perishes; but if untouchability is eradicated from the Hindu heart root and branch, then Hinduism has a definite message for the world. I have said the first thing to hundreds of audiences, but not the latter part. Now that is the utterance of a man who accepts Truth as God. It is therefore no exaggeration. If untouchability is an integral part of Hinduism, the latter is a spent bullet. But untouchability is a hideous untruth. My motive in launching the untouchability campaign is clear. What I am aiming at is not every Hindu touching an 'untouchable', but every touchable Hindu driving untouchability from his heart, going through a complete change of heart. Interdining or intermarrying is not the point. I may not dine with you, but I ought not to harbour the feeling that if I dined with you I should be polluted. If I was a woman to be married, I should not say, 'I cannot marry a man because he is an untouchable.' I am making this clear to you because in the programme of the Harijan Sevak Sangh we say we don't ask the orthodox Hindus to interdine or intermarry with the 'untouchables'. Many of us have no scruples about interdining or intermarriage. That untouchability is an ancient custom I admit, but there are many such things intertwined with Hinduism because it is an ancient religion, even a prehistoric religion. Instead of being the dead faith that it threatens to be, I want it to be a living faith, so that it may exist side by side with other religions of the world."

With this he explained the genesis of the Harijan Sevak Sangh, and how he could not be a member of the Sangh, and yet that he had directed and guided the policy of the Sangh.

"The world looks upon you," said Dr. Mott, "as a front-line prophet, conscience, initiator and warrior, and we pray that you may be spared long for this most fateful period in the life of the world."

*The Yeravda Pact*

The conversation led to the genesis of the Yeravda Pact, beginning with Gandhiji's declaration at the Round Table Conference, to lay down his life to stop the vivisection of Hinduism. "But," said Gandhiji, "I had no political axe to grind, I have none. Nor have the other Hindus a political motive. For instance the Pact has been a kind of bombshell thrown in the midst of Bengalis. They have their own Hindu-Muslim problem which has been rendered difficult by the Yeravda Pact. The original Premier's 'Award', as it was called, gave fewer seats to the

Harijans than the Pact gives. It is almost an overwhelming number. But I said Hinduism loses nothing if *all* the seats were captured by the Harijans. I would not alter a comma in the Pact unless the Harijans themselves wanted it."

Dr. Mott: "Removal of untouchability is the business of your lifetime. The importance of this movement lies beyond the frontiers of India, and yet there are few subjects on which there is more confusion of thought. Take for instance the Missionaries and Missionary Societies. They are not of one mind. It is highly desirable that we become of one mind and find out how far we can help and not hinder. I am Chairman of the International Missionary Council which combines 300 Missionary Societies in the world. I have on my desk reports of these societies, and I can say that their interest in the untouchables is deepening. I should be interested if you would feel free to tell me where, if anywhere, the Missionaries have gone along wrong lines. Their desire is to help and not to hinder."

*Deeply Hurt*

Gandhiji: "I cannot help saying that the activities of the Missionaries in this connection have hurt me. They with the Mussalmans and the Sikhs came forward as soon as Dr. Ambedkar threw the bombshell, and they gave it an importance out of all proportion to the weight it carried, and then ensued a rivalry between these organizations. I could understand the Muslim organizations doing this, as Hindus and Muslims have been quarrelling. The Sikh intervention is an enigma. But the Christian Mission claims to be a purely spiritual effort. It hurt me to find Christian bodies vying with the Muslims and Sikhs in trying to add to the numbers of their fold. It seemed to me an ugly performance and a travesty of religion. They even proceeded to enter into secret conclaves with Dr. Ambedkar. I should have understood and appreciated your prayers for the Harijans, but instead you made an appeal to those who had not even the mind and intelligence to understand what you talked; they have certainly not the intelligence to distinguish between Jesus and Muhammad and Nanak and so on."

Dr. Mott referred to the Archbishop of Canterbury's speech, and the talks he had with him, and other bishops and Missionary leaders in England, and emphasized the fact that the Christians should in no way seem to be bidding with others for the souls of the Indian people. He said he had a reassurance from the free as well as the State church leaders, but in the secular papers it had got abroad that Dr. Ambedkar could hand over 50 million people to those who were prepared to accept them. He had sensed that it might mean a tremendous disservice. "The most trustworthy leaders of Protestant Missionary forces," said Dr. Mott, "would give what you have said great heed. They do believe increasingly in work for the untouchables. Tell us what we can wisely do and what we cannot wisely do."

Gandhiji: "So far as this desire of Dr. Ambedkar is concerned, you can look at the whole movement with utter calmness and indifference. If there is any answer to Dr. Ambedkar's appeal and if the Harijans and he take the final step and come to you, you can take such steps as your conscience suggests. But today it seems unseemly and precipitate to anticipate what Dr. Ambedkar and Harijans are going to do."

*Deplorable*

Deenabandhu Andrews referred with condemnation to the Lucknow Conference, and Dr. Mott said that what the Conference did was not authoritative.

Gandhiji: It becomes authoritative owing to the silence of Christian bodies. If they had disowned all that happened, it would have been well, but those who met at Lucknow perhaps felt that they were voicing the views of the Missionary bodies who, in their opinion, were not moving fast enough.

Dr. Mott: But there was a disclaimer.

Gandhiji: If there was, it did not travel beyond the English Channel.

Dr. Mott: But there is a deplorable confusion of thought and divided counsel even amongst friends. The Devil would like nothing better. My life has been mostly spent for the intellectual classes, and I feel very much conscience-moved to help in this movement.

*Discard the Ulterior Motive*

Gandhiji cited the example of good Christians helping by working under the Hindu banner. There was Mr. Keithan who was trying hard to smooth the path of the untouchables. There were Miss Barr and Miss Madden who had thrown themselves into the Rural Reconstruction Movement. He then adverted to the problem in Travancore where an indecent competition was going on for enticing away the Ezhavas from the Hindu fold. "The Ezhavas in Travancore want temple entry. But it is no use your asking me wheher they want temple entry. Even if they do not want it, I must see that they enjoy the same rights as I enjoy, and so the reformers there are straining every nerve to open the temple doors. [Curiously enough this talk was taking place exactly at the moment when the Travancore Proclamation was being issued!]

Dr. Mott: But must we not serve them?

Gandhiji: Of course you will, but not make conversion the price of your service.

Dr. Mott: I agree that we ought to serve them whether they become Christians or not. Christ offered no inducements. He offered service and sacrifice.

Gandhiji: If Christians want to associate themselves with this reform movement, they should do so without any idea of conversion.

Dr. Mott: Apart from this unseemly competition, should they not preach the Gospel with reference to its acceptance?

Gandhiji: Would you, Dr. Mott, preach the Gospel to a cow? Well some of the untouchables are worse than cows in understanding. I mean they can no more distinguish between the relative merits of Islam and Hinduism and Christianity than can a cow. You can only preach through your life. The rose does not say: 'Come and smell me.'

Dr. Mott: But Christ said: 'Preach and Teach,' and also that Faith cometh by hearing, and hearing by the word of God. There was a day when I was an unbeliever. Then J. E. K. Studd of Cambridge, a famous cricketer, visited my University on an evangelistic mission and cleared the air for me. His life and splendid example alone would not have answered my question and met my deepest need, but I listened to him and was converted. First and foremost we must live the life; but then by wise and sympathetic unfolding of essential truth we must shed light on processes and actions and attitudes, and remove intellectual difficulties so that it may lead us into the freedom which is freedom indeed. You do not want the Christians to withdraw tomorrow?

Gandhiji: No. But I do not want you to come in the way of our work, if you cannot help us.

Dr. Mott: The whole Christian religion is the religion of sharing our life, and how can we share without supplementing our lives with words?

Gandhiji: Then what they are doing in Travancore is correct? There may be a difference of degree in what you say and what they are doing, but there is no difference of quality. If you must share it with the Harijans, why don't you share it with me, Thakkarbapa and Mahadev? Why should you go to the 'untouchables' and try to exploit this upheaval? Why not come to us instead?

Dr. Mott: The whole current discussion since the Ambedkar declaration has become badly mixed with other unworthy motives, which must be eliminated. Jesus said: 'Ye shall be witnesses unto Me.' A good Christian has to testify what he has experienced in his own life or as a result of his own observation. We are not true as His followers, if we are not true witnesses of Christ. He said: 'Go and teach and help through the mists and lead them out into larger light.'

Deenabandhu Andrews here asked to be permitted to put forward a concordat. He said: There are fundamental differences between you and the Missionaries, and yet you are the friend of Missionaries. But you feel that they are not playing the game. You want the leaders of the Church to say: 'We do not want to fish in troubled waters; we shall do nothing to imply that we are taking advantage of a peculiar situation that has arisen.'

Gandhiji: I do not think it is a matter which admits of any compromise at all. It is a deeply religious problem, and each should do what he likes. If your conscience tells you that the present effort is your mission, you need not give any quarter to Hindu reformers. I can simply state my belief that what the Missionaries are doing today does not show spirituality.

This merely is a gist of the long talk on the first day. At Gandhiji's invitation Dr. Mott came along the next morning for another talk. There is no room for it this week.

***Harijan*, 19-12-'36** M. D.

## 21

# DR. MOTT'S VISIT

## II

The next day's talk covered a variety of subjects, some of them of a deeply personal character. Introspection has played a great part in Dr. Mott's life, and he wanted to know the great forces that had been at work in shaping Gandhiji's personality. This talk seemed to bring them much closer to each other.

*Object of Stay in Sevagram*

Here is Dr. Mott's first question:

*Q*. What are the governing ideals and aims of this Indian village industries movement? What is the object of your settling down in this little village?

*A*. The immediate object of my stay here is to remove to the best of my ability the appalling ignorance, poverty and the still more appalling insanitation of the Indian villages. All these really run into one another. We seek to remove ignorance not through imparting the knowledge of the alphabet by word of mouth, but by giving them object-lessons in sanitation, by telling them what is happening in the world, and so on.

*Q*. What you are doing here has great industrial significance. Japan with about as high a rate of literacy as any country in the world is not exempt from the sins of industrialism.

*A*. But I am not seeking to industrialize the village. I want to revive the village after the ancient pattern, i.e. to revive hand-spinning, hand-ginning, and its other vital handicrafts. The village uplift movement is an offshoot of the spinning movement. So great was my ignorance in 1908 that I mixed up the spinning wheel with the loom in my small book on Indian Home Rule.* (With this Gandhiji

* *Hind Swaraj or Indian Home Rule,* Pub. Navajivan, Ahmedabad-14.

described the beginnings of the revival of the spinning wheel and explained the genesis of the Harijan movement and the All India Village Industries movement.)

*Gandhiji's Heaviest Burden*

Dr. Mott's next question was: What is the cause of your greatest concern, your heaviest burden?

Gandhiji: My greatest worry is the ignorance and poverty of the masses of India, and the way in which they have been neglected by the classes, especially the neglect of the Harijans by the Hindus. This criminal neglect is unwarranted by any of the scriptures. We are custodians of a great religion, and yet we have been guilty of a crime which constitutes our greatest shame. Had I not been a believer in the inscrutable ways of Providence, a sensitive man like me would have been a raving maniac.

Dr. Mott: What affords you the greatest hope and satisfaction?

Gandhiji: Faith in myself born of faith in God.

Dr. Mott: In moments when your heart may sink within you, you hark back to this faith in God?

Gandhiji: Yes. That is why I have always described myself as an irrepressible optimist.

Dr. Mott: So am I. Our difficulties are our salvation. They make us hark back to the living God.

Gandhiji: Yes. My difficulties have strengthened my faith which rises superior to every difficulty, and remains undimmed. My darkest hour was when I was in Bombay a few months ago. It was the hour of my temptation. Whilst I was asleep I suddenly felt as though I wanted to see a woman. Well a man who had tried to rise superior to the sex-instinct for nearly 40 years was bound to be intensely pained when he had this frightful experience. I ultimately conquered the feeling, but I was face to face with the blackest moment of my life and, if I had succumbed to it, it would have meant my absolute undoing. I was stirred to the depths because strength and peace come from a life of continence. Many Christian friends are jealous of the peace I possess. It comes from God who has blessed me with the strength to battle against temptation.

*The Darkest Hour*

Dr. Mott: I agree. 'Blessed are the pure in heart, for they shall see God.'

The talk now was switched on to subjects vastly different—those of current politics and other subjects. But Gandhiji would not allow a discussion on current politics in the columns of *Harijan*. I am therefore reluctantly obliged to omit this very important part of the discussion.

*The Place of Money*

Dr. Mott: If money is to be given to India, in what ways can it be wisely given without causing any harm? Will money be of any value?

Gandhiji: No. When money is *given* it can only do harm. It has got to be earned when it is required. I am convinced that the American and British money which has been voted for Missionary Societies has done more harm than good. You cannot serve God and Mammon both. And my fear is that Mammon has been sent to serve India and God has remained behind, with the result that He will one day have His vengeance. When the American says: 'I will serve you through money,' I dread him. I simply say to him: 'Send us your engineers not to earn money but to give us the benefit of their scientific knowledge.'

Dr. Mott: But money is stored-up personality. It can be badly used as well as well used. Through money you can get the services of a good engineer. But far more dangerous than money is human personality. It makes possible the good as well as the bad use of money. Kagawa of Japan admits that the use of money and machinery is attended with peril, but insists, and I agree with him, that Christ is able to dominate both the money and the machine.

Gandhiji: I have made the distinction between

money *given* and money *earned*. If an American says he wants to serve India, and you packed him off here, I should say we had not earned his services. But take Pierre Ceresole who came at his own expense, but after our consent, to serve earthquake-stricken Bihar. We would love to have as many Ceresoles as could possibly come to our help. No. It is my certain conviction based on experience that money plays the least part in matters of spirit.

Dr. Mott: If money is the root of evil, we are living in a time when there is more money than ever was before.

Gandhiji: Which means that there is more evil in the world.

Dr. Mott: This makes it supremely important that we study more profoundly than ever how to dominate this power both among the rich and the poor with spiritual purpose, motive and passion.

But they would have argued on and on this topic without coming to an agreement. They ultimately agreed to differ.

*Power of Silence*

The talk was now coming to an end. Dr. Mott laid his finger on one of the main sources of Gandhiji's strength. "The greatest thing you have ever done is the observance of your Monday silence. You illustrate thereby the storing up and releasing of power when needed. What place has it continued to have in the preparation of your spiritual tasks?" asked Dr. Mott.

"It is not the greatest thing I have done, but it certainly means a great thing to me," said Gandhiji. "I am now taking silence almost every day. If I could impose on myself silence for more days in the week than one, I should love it. In Yeravda Jail I once observed a 15 days' silence. I was in the seventh heaven during that period. But this silence is now being utilized to get through arrears of work. It is a superficial advantage after all. The real silence should not be interrupted even by writing notes to others and carrying on conversation through them. The notes interrupt the sacredness of the silence when you should listen to the music of the spheres. That is why I often say that my silence is a fraud."

*Harijan*, 26-12-'36 M. D.

22

# DR. MOTT'S SECOND VISIT

## I

*A Doughty Veteran*

Gandhiji's time has been full with visits from a number of Christian Missionaries who are in India to attend the forthcoming conference at Tambaram (Madras). Among these was also Dr. Mott who is to preside at the conference.

Some of the readers of *Harijan* will remember Dr. Mott's visit to Sevagram in December 1936 and my two articles thereon. I prefaced them with a brief sketch of the life and work of the great evangelist as a sort of background to the conversations between Dr. Mott and Gandhiji. In this preface I shall mention a few more facts.

His visit again to Sevagram after exactly two years serves but to strengthen the impression one gained of his personality. He is now 73, but he has lost none of his old vigour, and as he knows the secret of a well-regulated life one may hope that he will easily finish a century of fruitful life. Son of a big lumberman and meant for a legal career, he refused to choose either of the two careers and early made up his mind to dedicate every power of his body and mind to "incessant battle across the world, through decade after decade, for the Kingdom of God." In his tireless pursuit of his mission he has declined big secular positions. He was offered the Presidency of Princeton University when Woodrow Wilson resigned the post and later became

President of the United States. He was offered by President Wilson the post of the Ambassador for China. This too he declined and he has gone from one end of the earth to the other to unite Christianity. With characteristic precision and love of figures his biographer counts the number of countries he has visited and the miles he has covered. "At a conservative estimate," wrote Mr. Basil Mathews in 1934, "the total of Dr. Mott's journeying reaches 1,700,000 miles, or the equivalent of fully sixty-eight times round the world. His actual journeys round the world have been four." Creator of the World's Student Christian Federation, and its General Secretary for many years, he has also long been Chairman of the International Missionary Council and President of the World's Alliance of the Y. M. C. A. Throughout his long life he has been a student, predominantly in the interests of his mission to which every one of his waking hours is dedicated, and with that sole purpose he has visited and endeavoured to know and understand the workings of the minds of men like Tolstoy and Masaryk, Gandhiji and Kerensky, has addressed millions of students of all faiths, and made a point of visiting all important shrines of every faith, with a view to study the appeal behind every one of those faiths. A tremendous organizer, he has sustained helpful relations with many organizations for social, educational and religious betterment throughout the world, and his biographer says that "within a period stretching over forty years he sustained a relation of major responsibility toward raising a sum conservatively estimated at 300 million dollars for Christian and philanthropic work in every continent and nearly every nation on earth." Rigidly simple and abstemious in his habits from his childhood, he has loved to spread throughout the student world the gospel of a pure and dedicated life. His life of clock-like regularity allows him time to attend personally to his vast correspondence, to maintain a regular diary of his daily tasks, of books he has read and men and places he has seen.

*No Advance in Action*

When Dr. Mott came to Sevagram two years ago he confined himself almost exclusively to the question of "the 'untouchables' in India and how the Missionaries could help rather than hinder Gandhiji's task of the removal of the blot." The discussion ended with Gandhiji's emphatic assertion, based on evidence in his possession, that "what the Missionaries are doing today does not show spirituality." Dr. Mott agreed that the ulterior motive should be always discarded and that true Missionaries should serve people, "whether they become Christians or not". But he insisted on the liberty "to preach and teach". Gandhiji held that preaching and teaching could be best done through one's *life* which alone should be allowed to speak, that there should be no preaching *at* people but *to* people who sought light and guidance from you, and lastly, that it should be addressed to people who could understand.

Dr. Mott did not reopen these fundamental questions during this visit, but wondered if the world, including the world of Missionaries, had advanced since they had last met. He was going to preside over the deliberations of the International Missionary Council meeting in Madras during the month, and he wanted to share with Gandhiji the plans of the meeting, and wanted Gandhiji's "intuition and judgment on things to be discussed at the Convention". In his graceful way he said: "I have thanked God with every remembrance of you, and have always felt that you were never more needed than at this hour. I look upon you as a prophet and warrior, and you have appealed wonderfully even to people who have not seen you. We are confronted with possibly the most fateful period in history, and we want to our aid all the influence that God has given you. The conviction is growing on me that our many and taxing problems can best be solved in an international context. The world would seem to have been humbled since we last met. The conscience of the world is trembling, there is a world-wide awareness and desire that we should in this ever-shrinking world get closer together, and that is why I am again in India—India which has got more to teach us than any other country, not excepting China."

"India," he added, "is a land of great faiths and marvellous heritage and traditions, and we want all the help we can get. This is a unique Convention where 14 councils of the younger Churches of Asia, Africa and Latin America, and 14 of the older Churches of Europe, America and Australasia will be represented by over 400 delegates. We want this to be a help and not a hindrance to India. I have always been inspired by the unique, distinctive and God-implanted contribution of your writings in *Harijan*, and I have come to seek your guidance. Am I, I ask, right in thinking that the tide has turned a little bit on the great things you impressed on me? *First* was the matter of the Communal Award and the perils of it, that you vividly brought before me for Christianity in India. *Second* was the great danger of the Christian movement, in connection with the propagation of its faith, taking advantage of the disabilities of people, in order to augment the number of its adherents. *Third* was the question of the wise use of money. We have had a scientific study made of the economic basis of the Church in Asia and Africa. *Fourth* was the question of untouchability. It is not confined to India. It is inside some of the so-called Churches, and in Germany it is practised with reference to the Jews and in America with reference to the coloured people. Now this is what I want to know. Is there not a turning of the tide? Is there not a clearer recognition of these evils? Have we been going the right way on these problems?"

Gandhiji: What I have noticed is that there is a drift in the right direction so far as thought is concerned, but I do feel that in action there is *no* advance. I was going to say 'not much advance', but I deliberately say '*no* advance'.

You may be able to give solitary instances of men here and there, but they do not count. Right conviction to be of use has to be translated into action.

Dr. Mott: Take the first question, viz. that of the Communal Award. Has there been no progress?

Gandhiji: No progress at all.

Dr. Mott: I have been studying the manuscript of the life of K. T. Paul, to which I have been asked to write a foreword. Don't you think there has been an advance since his time? The attitude of the Roman Catholics is hostile, but what about Protestant Christians?

Gandhiji: If Protestant Christians are at one on this question, they can have the award changed, so far as they are concerned. But there is no solid action in the matter.

Dr. Mott: I did not know that they could have an exception made in their behalf.

Gandhiji: They can.

Dr. Mott: Take the next question. Is not taking advantage of people's disabilities being avoided now? I must say I was terribly pained to read of the Mc Gavran incident and greatly relieved to know that the misunderstanding has been cleared up.

Gandhiji: Even on this question, whilst some friends, I agree, are in earnest, so far as action goes there has been no change.

Dr. Mott: You mean to say there is not action *enough*?

Gandhiji: No, there is *no* action at all. I have plenty of evidence to prove what I say. I do not publish all the correspondence I get. Mr. A. A. Paul, whom you may know, convened a conference some time ago. The proceedings were revealing. Their resolutions were half-hearted. As far as I am aware, there was no unanimity about any definite action.

Dr. Mott: I was encouraged by a resolution of the National Christian Council which insisted on pure motives and pure practice.

Gandhiji: You may cite the resolution, but you will not be able to show corresponding action.

Dr. Mott: I understand. Without action no decision is anything worth. This lesson was burnt into my mind even as a student when Foster's great essay on the *Decision of Character* helped me more than anything I had read.

Gandhiji: I assure you you will find confirmation of what I say. I would say that there is not even concrete recognition of the danger of taking an undue advantage of people's disabilities. They will never give up what they call the right of mass conversions.

Dr. Mott: They are now talking of conversion of groups and families. I am not quite clear, though, as to what in certain cases the word "group" implies.

Gandhiji: I am quite clear. It is mass conversions called by another name.

Dr. Mott: That is strange. How can groups or families be converted *en masse*? Conversion in my family, for instance, came first with my father, then my oldest sister, then youngest sister, then I. It is an individual matter, a matter entirely between one and one's God.

Gandhiji: So it is. On this matter of untouchability, I may tell you that for years I could not carry conviction to my own wife. She followed me willynilly. The conviction came to her after long experience and practice.

Dr. Mott: In dealing with the holiest of things we should use the purest methods. But you will pardon me if I reiterate that I am hopeful of the tide having turned. Discerning Christian leaders to my knowledge are not only thinking of these things keenly but sincerely addressing themselves to fostering right practice.

Dr. Mott: On the third question of the wise use of money I see signs of encouragement.

Gandhiji: But it is a virtue of necessity. The Indian Christians are thinking aloud and of doing things themselves. They are talking of their own responsibilities and saying, "Thank God, American money can't come."

[Then came a rather long digression on the wise and unwise use of money. The topic had engaged their attention on the occasion of the last visit too, and Gandhiji had put the matter most forcefully when he said: "I think that you cannot serve God and Mammon both, and my fear is that Mammon has been sent to serve India and God has remained behind, with the result that He will one day have His vengeance." He had made it also clear that there was all the difference in the world between money *given* and money *earned*.]

Dr. Mott: But your own example proves that there are wise uses of money. What do all the organizations I saw this morning testify?

Gandhiji: You see a contradiction between my theory and practice? Well, you must see the background. With all my experience and ability to collect money I am utterly indifferent in the matter. I have always felt that when a religious organization has more money than it requires, it is in peril of losing its faith in God and pinning its faith on money. There is no such thing as *wise* or *unwise* use of money. You have simply to cease to depend on it. You don't even depend on bread, and bargain with God saying you won't pray until God gives you bread!

Dr. Mott: I am arguing this at some length as I want to understand you and not to misquote you.

Gandhiji: Then I will illustrate what I say by two telling illustrations. In South Africa when I started the Satyagraha march there was not a copper in my pocket, and I went with a light heart. I had a caravan of 3,000 people to support. 'No fear,' said I. 'If God wills it, He will carry it forward.' Then money began to rain from India. I had to stop it, for when the money came my miseries began. Whereas they were content with a piece of bread and sugar, they now began asking for all sorts of things.

Then take the illustration of the new educational experiment. The experiment, I said, must go on without asking for any monetary help. Otherwise, after my death the whole organization would go to pieces. The fact is the moment financial stability is assured, spiritual bankruptcy is also assured.

Dr. Mott: But you wisely used the money.

Gandhiji: Not metal, but bread; and even the dog, under God's Providence, has not to go hungry.

[I may add, for the sake of Dr. Mott, that on this matter Gandhiji's view is derived from his vow of *aparigraha*—non-possession, which in substance means that 'you may have occasion to possess or use material things, but the secret of life lies in never missing them.' Money will come for an object to which you are prepared to give up your life, but when there is no money you will not miss it, and the object will be carried on, perhaps all the better for want of it.]

Then came the last question of untouchability. Dr. Mott wondered if there was no quickening of the conscience all the world over. There had been, he said, battles royal between groups in America, conventions refusing to go to hotels where the Negroes were not received, there were Christians in Germany who had gone to prison for protesting against the inhuman treatment of the Jews. There was gold coming out of dross. What about India?

Gandhiji: No advance in action, I say again. The British are a fair test. The racial feeling instead of declining is rising. In South Africa the tide of prejudice is rising high, declarations made by former Ministers are being disregarded. Similar stories come from East Africa. But I remain an optimist, not that there is any evidence that I can give that right is going to prosper, but because of my unflinching faith that right must prosper in the end.

Dr. Mott: Well, in South Africa too are there not people like Hoffmeyr and Edgar Brookes? There is certainly a turn of the tide on the part of certain individuals.

Gandhiji: It would be wrong to draw conclusions from a handful of individual instances. Our inspiration can come only from our faith that right must ultimately prevail. But on this matter, as I have said, there is an advance in the thought world, but not in action.

Dr. Mott then insisted that most of the great advances of the human race were traceable to the initiative of individuals who had courageously and sacrificially made unpopular causes popular and triumphant.

## II

### *How to Fight National Gangsterism?*

Dr. Mott began the next day with these prefatory remarks: "You put in your quite original way your views on the questions I asked. I value it more than I can say. I was impressed by your recognition that there was a certain amount of advance in thought but not in action. It is a great thing that so many leading minds have begun to think about these vital questions in an advanced way. I could show you, too, that there are certain things actually concretely on foot. But today I want to engage your attention on another matter. What to do with 'gangster' nations, if I may use the expression frequently used? There was individual gangsterism in America. It has been put down by strong police measures both local and national. Could not we do some thing similar for gangsterism between nations, as instanced in Manchuria—the nefarious use of the opium poison—, in Abyssinia, in Spain, in the sudden seizure of Austria, and then in the case of Czechoslovakia. Now, in this connection, let me say, I was deeply impressed by what you wrote on the Czechoslovakian crisis and on the Jewish question. Can we bring something like international police into being?

Gandhiji: This question is not new to me.

Dr. Mott: I judge not.

Gandhiji: I have to deal with identical questions with reference to conditions in India. We have had to quell riots, communal and labour. The Ministries have used military force in some cases and police in most. Now whilst I agreed that the ministers could not help doing so, I also said that the Congress Ministries had proved themselves bankrupt with their stock-in-trade, I mean their avowed weapon of non-violence. Even so, I would say in reply to the question you have asked, viz. that, if the best mind of the world has not imbibed the spirit of non-violence, they would have to meet gangsterism in the orthodox way. But that would only show that we have not got far beyond the Law of the Jungle, that we have not yet learnt to appreciate the heritage that God has given us, that in spite of the teaching of Christianity which is 1900 years old and of Hinduism and Buddhism which are older, and even of Islam (if I have read it aright), we have not made much headway as human beings. But whilst I would understand the use of force by those who have not the spirit of non-violence in them, I would have those who know non-violence to throw their whole weight in demonstrating that even gangsterism has to be met by non-violence. For, ultimately, force, however justifiably used, will lead us into the same morass as the force of Hitler and Mussolini. There will be just a difference of degree. You and I who believe in non-violence must use it at the critical moment. We may not despair of touching the heart even of gangsters, even if, for the moment, we may seem to be striking our heads against a blind wall.

*How May Missionaries Help?*

Dr. Mott's next question was, "How may the

Missionaries and Christians in general help in constructive activities like the village industries movement, the new educational movement, and so on?"

Gandhiji gave some personal reminiscences which I omit. The substance of what he said was: "They should study the movements and work under, or in co-operation with, these organizations. I am happy to be able to say that I have some valued Christian colleagues. But they can be counted on one's fingers. I fear that the vast bulk of them remain unconvinced. Some have frankly said that they do not believe in the village movement or the education movement as they are conducted by the associations you have named. They evidently believe in industrialization and the Western type of education. And the Missionaries as a body perhaps fight shy of movements not conducted wholly or predominantly by Christians. If I get in my activities the hearty and active co-operation of the 5,000 Protestant Missionaries in India, and if they really believe in the living power of non-violence as the only force that counts, they can help not only here but perhaps in affecting the West."

Dr. Mott: Happily there are a goodly number amongst them who see eye to eye with you.

Gandhiji: I know.

Dr. Mott: I think the Congress movement has great force and every Missionary should consider how he can be most helpful in it.

*Creative Experiences*

Dr. Mott next asked a few personal questions. "What have been the most creative experiences in your life? As you look back on your past, what, do you think, led you to believe in God when everything seemed to point to the contrary, when life, so to say, sprang from the ground, although it all looked impossible?"

Gandhiji: Such experiences are a multitude. But as

you put the question to me, I recalled particularly one experience that changed the course of my life. That fell to my lot seven days after I had arrived in South Africa. I had gone there on a purely mundane and selfish mission. I was just a boy returned from England wanting to make some money. Suddenly the client who had taken me there asked me to go to Pretoria from Durban. It was not an easy journey. There was the railway journey as far as Charlestown and the coach to Johannesburg. On the train I had a first class ticket, but not a bed ticket. At Maritzburg where the beddings were issued the guard came and turned me out and asked me to go to the van compartment. I would not go, and the train steamed away leaving me shivering in the cold. Now the creative experience comes there. I was afraid for my very life. I entered the dark waiting room. There was a white man in the room. I was afraid of him. What was my duty, I asked myself. Should I go back to India, or should I go forward, with God as my helper, and face whatever was in store for me? I decided to stay and suffer. My active non-violence began from that date. And God put me through the test during that very journey. I was severely assaulted by the coachman for my not moving from the seat he had given me.*

Dr. Mott: The miseries, the slaps after slaps you received burnt into your soul.

Gandhiji: Yes, that was one of the richest experiences of my life.

Dr. Mott: I am grateful to you for sharing this experience with me.

*God Appears in Action*

Dr. Mott: What has brought deepest satisfaction to your soul in difficulties and doubts and questionings?

*For a detailed description of this incident read Gandhiji's *Autobiography*, Part II, Chs. VIII-IX. Pub. Navajivan, Ahmedabad-14

Gandhiji: Living faith in God.

Dr. Mott: When have you had indubitable manifestation of God in your life and experiences?

Gandhiji: I have seen and believe that God never appears to you in person, but in action which can only account for your deliverance in your darkest hour.

Dr. Mott: You mean things take place that cannot possibly happen apart from God.

Gandhiji: Yes. They happen suddenly and unawares. One experience stands quite distinctly in my memory. It relates to my 21 days' fast for the removal of untouchability. I had gone to sleep the night before without the slightest idea of having to declare a fast the next morning. At about 12 o'clock in the night something wakes me up suddenly, and some voice—within or without, I cannot say —whispers, 'Thou must go on a fast.' 'How many days?' I ask. The voice again says, 'Twenty-one days.' 'When does it begin?' I ask. It says, 'You begin tomorrow.' I went quietly off to sleep after making the decision. I did not tell anything to my companions until after the morning prayer. I placed into their hands a slip of paper announcing my decision and asking them not to argue with me, as the decision was irrevocable. Well, the doctors thought I would not survive the fast. But something within me said that I would, and that I must go forward. That kind of experience has never in my life happened before or after that date.

Dr. Mott: Now, you surely can't trace such a thing to an evil source?

Gandhiji: Surely not. I never have thought it was an error. If ever there was in my life a spiritual fast, it was this. There is something in denying satisfaction of the flesh. It is not possible to see God face to face unless you crucify the flesh. It is one thing to do what belongs to it as a temple of God, and it is another to deny it what belongs to it as to the body of flesh.

*Silence*

Dr. Mott concluded his visit in 1936 with a question on silence. He had done so during a brief flying visit to Ahmedabad in 1928, and during this visit too he asked if Gandhiji had continued to find it necessary in his spiritual quest.

Gandhiji: I can say that I am an everlastingly silent man now. Only a little while ago I have remained completely silent nearly two months, and the spell of that silence has not yet broken. I broke it today when you came. Nowadays I go into silence at prayer time every evening and break it for visitors at 2 o'clock. I broke it today when you came. It has now become both a physical and spiritual necessity for me. Originally it was taken to relieve the sense of pressure. Then I wanted time for writing. After, however, I had practised it for some time I saw the spiritual value of it. It suddenly flashed across my mind that that was the time when I could best hold communion with God. And now I feel as though I was naturally built for silence. Of course I may tell you that from my childhood I have been noted for my silence. I was silent at school, and in my London days I was taken for a silent drone by friends.

Dr. Mott: In this connection you put me in mind of two texts from the Bible:

"My soul, be thou silent unto God."

"Speak Lord, for Thy servant hearkeneth."

I have often sought silence for communion even during my noisiest time. I have had recourse to sea voyages for this purpose, though of course the radio has now robbed even a sea voyage of the privilege of silence one used to enjoy on the boat. But silent prayer is not a monologue, but a dialogue, and God speaks to us only when we are silently ready to listen to Him.

But the time was up and there was a cluster of visitors already waiting. Dr. Mott therefore left, saying: "I am sorry to have overstayed my time. I lose all sense of time when I am with you. I am more grateful than I can say."

Segaon, 5-12-'38

*Harijan*, 10-12-'38 M. D.

## 23

## DR. KAGAWA'S VISIT

*His Reputation*

"Your reputation has preceded you, Dr. Kagawa." With these words Gandhiji stood up to greet Dr. Kagawa who fell on his knees to return the greeting. All of us had long been looking forward to his visit or to the meeting between Dr. Kagawa and Gandhiji. If times had been normal and conditions in India had permitted Gandhiji to go abroad, he would certainly have gone to Japan to see Dr. Kagawa and his work, just as he went to Switzerland to see M. Romain Rolland, and would have gone to Turkey to see Kemal Pasha if peremptory cables had not called him back to India from England in 1931.

"You are a youngster before me," said Gandhiji, when in reply to his question Dr. Kagawa said that he was 50 years and six months old. But what a crowded period of 50 years! And though he enjoys the same reputation with his people as Gandhiji does in India, what a study in comparison and contrast are the lives of the two! Toyohiko Kagawa was born in Kobe in 1888, the son of a headman of 19 villages, who later rose to a high position in the State. But he was born out of wedlock, as his biographer Mr. Axling says, or was the son of "a professional dancing girl", who was "my father's second wife" as Kagawa himself says in an autobiographical chapter in one of his famous books. "My father died when I was only four, and the first wife adopted me as her own. We had a big house and many servants. But living in a big house without any love meant hell for me. My family were rich people, but their mode of behaviour was terrible. I wept day and night." Dr. Kagawa said, as he was talking to me, that it was this polygamy in the family which drove him to Christianity. If I may say so, however, it was not polygamy, but the total lack of love. There is no lack of love in Buddhism, but there was a famine of pure love in the so-called Buddhist home. Even so, Dr. Ambedkar born in Hinduism experienced a total lack of love from his Hindu brethren and so swore enmity to Hinduism.

In Dr. Kagawa's early life there was no love, and there was no light. Buddhism was then, or seemed to him to be, no more than crude ritual, worship of the dead, which carried with them no obligation of love. The school which he attended offered no better atmosphere. "The senior students of the high school visited the licensed quarters of public prostitution and they got drunk. There seemed no hope for me to be a good boy." At this stage an American missionary came into his loveless and lightless life. He asked him to memorize the Sermon on the Mount, and the passage about the "lilies of the field" captivated him. "I believed that, if I could be like one of these lilies in the field, I could be a good boy. My uncle was very much against Christianity. He was an honest Buddhist. I could not confess my faith openly, so I used to pray in bed, putting the bedcovers over my head, 'O God, make me a good boy.' I went to the missionary to borrow some books....'How do you pray,' he asked. 'Under the covers at night,' I said. He laughed at me and said I was a coward. I did not like the word coward, so I went and for the first time worshipped God in Church. I received baptism."

After graduating he decided to serve the poor, as Christianity meant for him nothing else. He went and lived with the poor in hovels six feet square. These slums were bywords for blood and sin, but he feared neither murder nor syphilis, made murderers and dissolute men his bedfellows. With a thief, a murderer, a lunatic and a syphilitic for his mates he lived on "only eleven yen a day for four people. It is impossible to feed four people on eleven yen even in Japan. We skipped lunch and had two meals a day. We put water in the rice and we watered our stomachs. I preached to the drunkards at two o'clock, for that was the only time they were sober. I preached to the gamblers. I preached day and night, but the result was very bad, because when people go down to the slums they have no power to get higher."

Blackmailers exploited his non-resistance—he gave a coat and trousers to one who wanted a shirt—and a criminal knocked out his four front teeth. In his eyes he still carries signs of the disease he caught in the slums. After five years in the slums he went to America, studied biology and psychology at Princeton, took his doctorate in theology, and on return changed his tactics and organized labour unions. There was a big general strike; he was arrested with 450 labour leaders. In times of depression the workman is driven back to the land, and so Dr. Kagawa began to study the life of the workman returned to the land, and thus of the farmer. He was again arrested because he got one hundred and fifty thousand farmers to join the farmers' union. But all these years were not really "love's labour lost". In 1926 the Government, moved by his writings, sanctioned a sum of 2 million pounds to remove slums from six of the largest cities in Japan, and these are now free of such areas.

*His Grasp of Facts*

Dr. Kagawa had to fight the slums, the immorality, the poverty of the workman and the peasant. He has a marvellous mastery of figures. Here are some he quotes almost casually: "In Japan drink consumes fifty per cent more money than the total annual budget of the army and navy....It is estimated that money spent in licensed and private prostitution in Japan amounts to 1,000 million yen annually. Significantly the annual consumption of rice amounts to 1,500 million yen or only one-half as much more." (*Brotherhood Economics.*) "In Japan we have 140 large cities, and 1,200 towns and villages are rural. Only 48 per cent of the total population is rural. We have three million fishermen in Japan, and they catch half the fish that are caught in the whole world....We have 8,600 storages for rice based on the co-operative scheme.... 40 per cent of the 5,700,000 farmers are landless. 30 per cent of them have a little land, 70 per cent are tenant farmers; 28 per cent are owners owning small lands; only 2 per cent of the farmers are well off. 65 per cent of the owners of farms live in the towns and cities." (Speech at the Tambaram conference.) "There are 5,700,000 families of farmers in Japan....Yet we have only 300,000 Christians in the Church." (*Brotherhood Economics.*) This book from which I have taken this last quotation contains a brief and yet comprehensive account of the co-operative movement which is well worth studying by all social workers. Russian communism, he says, has evolved a system of forced co-operatives. What we need are voluntary co-operatives. "We may have no reason to love the capitalists as capitalists, but we must help them to repent and to co-operate with their fellows in a society which shall be based upon Christian brotherhood and love."

### *His Dream*

He demonstrates the need for seven types of co-operatives:

(1) Health insurance and life insurance co-operatives; (2) producers' co-operatives; (3) marketing co-operatives; (4) credit co-operatives; (5) mutual aid co-operatives; (6) utility co-operatives; and (7) consumers' co-operatives —which he calls the seven types of brotherhood.

He is himself running day nurseries under the co-operative system and two experimental stations in

Hokkaido (North Japan) and Tokio (South Japan), and under the inspiration of these stations every district has decided to grow 50,000 walnut trees and 100,000 chestnut trees every year.

He indulges in his dream of a "Co-operative State" based on the co-operatives and founded on Christlike redemptive love. He is a socialist but is opposed to violent confiscation, and thinks that the greatest problem "would be some method of transferring the system of private property over to a system of co-operative property." He rightly dreams of a system of elections of persons from co-ordinated organizations, which would obviate the necessity of expending money on elections, and ultimately talks of international co-operative trade and commerce to ensure peace. There are interesting discussions in the book on property and inheritance taxes, limits of private ownership and so on, and there is throughout an insistence on education and non-violent revolution as the "only true and dependable" method for the "emancipation of the proletariat". International co-operative trade, and internationalization of earthquake and flood insurance, just as there is the international postal treaty, would ensure world peace. "The whole question resolves itself into the education of the nations into the will to give expression to a co-operative spirit in the foundation of such international co-operative institutions as an international credit bank. Such institutions would mark a long step toward the achievement of world peace."

While that is his dream, I wonder if it has ever occurred to him that economic exploitation by Japan of other countries is contrary to the principle of love and brotherhood, that working for manufacture of munitions is also opposed to the same principle. He is not explicit in his views on war, especially the present Sino-Japanese war. He talks of the problem of over-population and complacently talks of a million families to be sent to the north of Manchukuo to be settled there. "How can there be international co-operative trade between an independent nation and a subject nation, between an exploiting nation and an exploited one?" I asked him. He said: "I agree that yours is a different problem altogether."

*A Query and an Explanation*

His attitude to conversion is well defined. He believes in a second birth—"Unless ye be born again." But inasmuch as birth cannot be a collective matter, he would not, so I think, countenance mass conversions. I tried in vain to carry him further than this. If Christ taught love and brotherhood, Buddha had taught Ahimsa and conquering evil by good. But, as I have explained, the life of Christ came first to inspire him, and he likes to visualize a universal church of Christ and the life of the Gospel. "But," I asked him, "why may one not live the life of love, or, if you please, life according to the Gospel, without being baptized?" He had no reply. "But of course," he said, "I do not believe in compulsion. When I talk to the Buddhist peasants and workers about co-operatives, I do not talk of religion. But if they do come to ask me about religion, I take the Gospel to them." He recognizes that the teachings of Christ are being challenged, and declares in no uncertain terms: "If the Church were trying to practise love in society, there would be a reason for its existence. With creeds alone I do not expect it to be able to save the world." But as we will see, he does not appear to have worked out his faith to its extreme logical conclusion. I may be mistaken, but it is my conviction that having cut himself adrift from his people in early life, he lacks the capacity to antagonize them on large issues out of the depth of love.

"Why has not pacifism made much headway?" we asked him. "Look at the mobilization law," he said. "You cannot speak, you cannot write what you please. Everyone under fifty has to enlist himself." "But," said I, "if you find thousands of men willing to throw themselves into the jaws of death for war, why can't you find thousands willing to go to death for their convictions, for peace?" He smiled incredulously.

I must confess that I do not fully understand Dr. Kagawa. His talk with Gandhiji on his own attitude to war had to be incomplete for want of time. There were peculiar difficulties of the situation which Dr. Kagawa might have discussed at length with Gandhiji. Japan is still a peculiarly feudal country. It is dominated by the militarist caste or by military cliques. No less than five Prime Ministers have been assassinated there during recent years. Luck has favoured the country and its militarist policy all these years. And it is not an easy matter to preach a heretical doctrine in such an atmosphere. Considerable educative propaganda is needed before the ground can be prepared. Besides, Buddhism as it has been understood and practised in India has not been so understood in Japan and other lands. These peculiar difficulties explain in a large measure Dr. Kagawa's position, his inability or his unpreparedness to clarify his attitude, and to live up to the extreme logical consequences of his creed.

*The Discourse with Gandhiji*

I have already described how they greeted each other. The preliminary questions were about the drought in South India and famines and the co-operative movement. Was the movement flourishing in India? Dr. Kagawa asked.

"I can't say that it is flourishing," said Gandhiji. "It is going on somehow. It was initiated by the British Government. It did not come from within, but was superimposed upon the people. It is managed after a certain stereotyped pattern and has therefore no room for growth according to the exigencies of time. Whereas I know you have a big co-operative movement."

"Yes, it is growing every day. There are 350,000 producers' co-operatives organized by themselves. There are national health insurance co-operatives, harvest insurance co-operatives and storage co-operatives," said Dr. Kagawa.

### *The War with China*

But that discussion could not enthuse Gandhiji. He went straight to the question on which he wanted to hear first hand from Dr. Kagawa. "What is the feeling of people in Japan about the war?"

"I am rather a heretic in Japan," said Dr. Kagawa. "Rather than I express my views, I would like to learn from you what you would do if you were in my position."

"It would be presumptuous for me to express my views."

"No, I would like very much to know what you would do."

"I would declare my heresies and be shot. I would put the co-operatives and all your work in one scale, and put the honour of your nation in the other, and if you found that the honour was being sold, I should ask you to declare your views against Japan and in so doing make Japan live through your death. But, for this, inner conviction is necessary. I do not know that I should be able to do all that I have said if I were in your position, but I must give you my opinion since you have asked for it."

"The conviction is there. But friends have been asking me to desist."

"Well, don't listen to friends when the Friend inside you says, 'Do this.' And friends, however good, can sometimes well deceive us. They cannot argue otherwise. They would ask you to *live* and do your work. The same appeal was made to me when I took the decision to go to jail. But I did not listen to friends with the result that I found the glow of freedom when I was confined within the four solid walls of prison. I was inside a dark cell, but I felt that I could see everything from within those walls, and nothing from outside."

Dr. Kagawa seemed to shrink from continuing this discussion. There was indeed no room for it. The conviction was there, but it could fructify only in its proper time. So he switched on again to his theme of co-operation: "Have you some irrigation co-operatives in India?" But Gandhiji was full of other things.

"I do not think so," Gandhiji replied. "Of course you have all these things. You have done marvellous things, and we have many things to learn from you. But how can we understand this swallowing alive of China, drugging her with poison and so many other horrid things that I read about in a book called *What War Means* which Pandit Jawaharlal has given me. How could you have committed all these atrocities? And then your great poet calls it a war of humanity and a blessing to China!"

*The Teaching of the Gita*

Dr. Kagawa is a student of religions. He wanted to know how Gandhiji's Ahimsa teaching could be reconciled with the Bhagavadgita. Gandhiji said it could not be discussed in a brief interval, but he would ask him to read his introduction to the Gita where he had answered the question. The answer had just come to him as part of his experience, and the interpretation was, as he thought, not laboured in any way.

Dr. Kagawa: I am told you recite the Bhagavadgita daily?

Gandhiji: Yes, we finish the entire Gita reading once every week.

Dr. Kagawa: But at the end of the Gita Krishna recommends violence.

Gandhiji: I do not think so. I am also fighting. I should not be fighting effectively if I were fighting violently. The message of the Gita is to be found in the second chapter of the Gita where Krishna speaks of the balanced state of mind, of mental equipoise. In 19 verses at the close of the 2nd chapter of the Gita Krishna explains how this state can be achieved. It can be achieved, he tells us, after killing all your passions. It is not possible to kill your brother after having killed all your passions. I should like to see that man dealing death—who has no passions, who is indifferent to pleasure and pain, who is undisturbed by the storms that trouble mortal man. The whole thing is described in language of beauty that is unsurpassed. These verses show that the fight Krishna speaks of is a spiritual fight.

Dr. Kagawa: But there was actual fighting then, and your interpretation is your own peculiar interpretation.

Gandhiji: It may be mine, but *as mine* it has no value.

Dr. Kagawa: To the common mind it sounds as though it was actual fighting.

Gandhiji: You must read the whole thing dispassionately in its true context. After the first mention of fighting, there is no mention of fighting at all. The rest is a spiritual discourse.

Dr. Kagawa: Has anybody interpreted it like you?

Gandhiji: Yes. The fight is there, but the fight as it is going on within. The Pandawas and Kaurawas are the forces of good and evil within. The war is the war between Jekyll and Hyde, God and Satan, going on in the human breast. The internal evidence in support of this interpretation is there in the work itself and in the Mahabharata of which the Gita is a minute part. It is not a history of war between two families, but the history of man—the history of the spiritual struggle of man. I have sound reasons for my interpretation.

Dr. Kagawa: That is why I say it is *your* interpretation.

Gandhiji: But that is nothing. The question is whether it is a reasonable interpretation, whether it carries conviction. If it does, it does not matter whether it is mine or X. Y. Z's. If it does not, it has no value even if it is mine.

Dr. Kagawa: To my mind Arjuna's ideas are wonderful. Krishna has found some excuse for him, and it was natural and necessary before Christianity.

Gandhiji: This interpretation is even historically wrong. For Buddha existed long before the Christian era, and he preached the doctrine of non-violence.

Dr. Kagawa: But Arjuna's views seem to me to be superior to Krishna's.

Gandhiji: Then according to you the disciple was greater than the master!

Dr. Kagawa: But I agree with what you say, with your teaching of non-violence. I shall read the Gita again, bearing your interpretation in mind.

Dr. Kagawa later told me that Arjuna's view was definitely right, and it was because he could not accept Krishna's teaching that he accepted the New Testament teaching as supreme. And yet curiously enough he also argued, when I tried to explain to him Lord Krishna's teaching, that the Japanese soldiers were fighting without passion or hatred in their breast! I also told him that the teaching of non-violence was at the root of the Hindu culture, that long before the Gita and even before Buddha the Vedic rishis had taught it, that Buddha derived his message from the Upanishads, and that Krishna delivered the same in a beautifully dramatic setting. Dr. Kagawa had read the Upanishads in the Sacred Books of the East Series but doubted where the teaching of Ahimsa came in. I urged him to read the Upanishads again.

*Change What?*

Dr. Kagawa again turned to his great theme—agriculture and co-operation which he had studied carefully. And indeed it is a pleasure to hear him discourse on methods of famine relief. "You get famine once in every *ten* years," he said. "We get it every year, famine is our constant friend," said Gandhiji. "Then," said Dr. Kagawa, "you should have more tree culture, more trees for fuel and for cattle fodder. Rice and barley are not enough, you need more protein trees." He particularly mentioned to me the Legumæ class trees for fuel (from China)—have not we our *babul* or *mimosa* which gives fuel and cattle-nuts both? —and he mentioned the Kiwave tree or the King tree from Hawaii which flowers three times in the year and yields 100 bushels of seed a year, sufficient to feed 25 horses. These grow in any soil and take 6 years to fruit. Having ensured animal-fodder, he said, the peasants should have more goats. The Japanese had successfully introduced two varieties from Sweden—the Saamen and the Toggenberg—which gave plenty of milk and hair, and which could live on scrub grass. In the Gobi desert they just evaporated goat's milk and lived on goat-milk cheese. Why should we in famine not fall back on goat-cheese and other milk products like the peasants in Mongolia? We badly needed to make a change in our methods of agriculture, said Dr. Kagawa.

"No," said Gandhiji laughing, "we need a change in the method of government!"

*What an Itinerary!*

It was a great pity that Dr. Kagawa had to go away to Bombay the same evening, and could not prolong his stay. Having only touched on fundamental questions, Gandhiji said he wished they had been together for hours or rather days. Dr. Kagawa swears by the method of non-violence. "To me *that* is the way, that is life. It is man's way, the other is Satan's way," he said. If that was the thing, it was no use hurrying through in the American way. Even for a detailed discussion of his co-operative programme he might have stayed longer with the leading men in India. But Gandhiji appealed to him on a different ground. "How can you leave India without seeing Santiniketan?" he asked.

Dr. Kagawa: But I have read the Poet's poems, and I love them.

Gandhiji: But you have to love the Poet.

Dr. Kagawa: If I can repeat the *Gitanjali* every day, I can see the Poet every day, and do I not love him? Maybe he is greater than his poems.

Gandhiji: Sometimes the reverse is the truth, but in the case of the Poet he is infinitely greater than his great poems. Now, another question. Have you included Pondicherry in your programme? If you want to study modern India, you must see both Santiniketan and Aravinda Ghose's Ashram. I wonder who your tour advisers are. I wish you had appointed me your adviser in this matter!

"No," said Dr. Kagawa laughing, "you are a good guide for life."

Dr. Kagawa asked what other books Gandhiji read every day. Gandhiji mentioned the Ramayana in which, he said, there was supposed to be enough blood and thunder, *"but not for me."* Dr. Kagawa said he too loved it for the story of Sita—the ideal of chastity. "But there are other fine things also in that unique poem," said Gandhiji. "I have not read the original which is great. But the Hindi rendering done by a great devotee is the scripture for the masses of India. In the North India Tulsi Ramayana has been the inspiration of many a home for four centuries."

Dr. Kagawa discussed Shankaracharya and Ramanuja, and Gandhiji expressed his predilection for the former, and for his direct and marvellously logical way. But Gandhiji reverted again to his itinerary, and expressed his great regret that Rev. Hodge who had been in charge of it had, out of his partiality for him (Gandhiji) included Bardoli, but not Santiniketan! "You are going to Calcutta and not to Santiniketan? It is a great pity. You say you are going to Gosaba. Well, Gosaba is Gosaba, but Santiniketan is India."

We appealed to Dr. Kagawa at the end of the interview to alter his programme a little. He was spending six days at Calcutta to see the Theological College at Serampur and

Sir Daniel Hamilton's Estate at Gosaba. Why not set apart a day for Santiniketan? Why not cut out other places and stay longer with Gandhiji? But it was an officially—or clerically?—arranged programme for him, and we could not help feeling very sad that his advisers had not been fair either to him or to India.

M. D.

*Harijan*, 21-1-'39

24

## MISSIONARIES ONCE AGAIN

If there is one thing that one can genuinely admire in the Missionaries, it is their persistence. They know what Gandhiji has to say in reply to their stock questions, but they go on asking them in the spirit of converting him or, I take it, being in their turn converted. A group of them saw him at Sevagram the other day. We were busy packing to go to Ramgarh, and there was hardly any time that Gandhiji could spare. But he promised to see them for five minutes. And they did indeed make the best of their time.

"What started you on your career of leadership?" was the queer question with which they started.

"It came to me, unsought, unasked," said Gandhiji rather embarrassed. "I do not know, though, what sort of leader I am, and whether what I am doing is leadership or service. But whatever it is, it came to me unasked."

But the friends who came were sure that they were leaders, and they asked for guidance as leaders of Christian thought.

"All I can say," said Gandhiji, "is that there should be less of theology and more of truth in all that you say and do."

"Will you kindly explain it?"

"How can I explain the obvious? Amongst agents of the many untruths that are propounded in the world one of the foremost is theology. I do not say that there is no demand for it. There is a demand in the world for many a questionable thing. But even those who have to do with theology as part of their work have to survive their theology. I have two good Christian friends who gave up theology and decided to live the gospel of Christ."

"Are you sure that no great result has come through your own study of Jesus?"

"Why? There is no doubt that it has come, but not, let me tell you, through theology or through the ordinary interpretation of theologists. For many of them contend that the Sermon on the Mount does not apply to mundane things, and that it was only meant for the twelve disciples. Well, I do not believe this. I think the Sermon on the Mount has no meaning if it is not of vital use in everyday life to everyone."

"Is there not to be found a solution of the present-day problems in the teaching of Jesus?"

"Well, you are now dragging me in deeper waters," exclaimed Gandhiji, "and you will drown me."

"What is the present trend of the thought of Young India?"

"It would take a brave and knowing man to answer this question. But," he smilingly said, "I must tell you that you have overstayed your time already. And if you go on questioning and cross-questioning me, I dare say you will floor me without being any the wiser for having done so."

*A Seeker*

Of a different type, so far as I could judge, was a Missionary friend who saw him long before this and asked him similar questions in a different spirit. He was more a seeker than a questioner. "Could you tell me the things one should avoid in order to present the gospel of Christ?" he asked.

"Cease to think that you want to convert the whole world to your interpretation of Christianity. At the end of reading the Bible, let me tell you, it did not leave on my mind the impression that Jesus ever meant Christians to do what the bulk of those who take his name do. The moment you adopt the attitude I suggest, the field of service becomes limitless. You limit your own capacity by thinking and saying that you must proselytize."

"I see what you mean," he said. "We have been cumbered by creeds and man-made things. We feel that we should be in a place where all barriers have broken down."

Gandhiji instanced a few Christians who, he said, saw the central fact that, if they wanted to live this Christian life, they should literally follow the words—"Not he that sayeth 'Lord, Lord,' but he that doeth His will."

"You are living a guided life. Could you kindly tell me your experience of guidance?"

"I do not regard God as a person," said Gandhiji. "Truth for me is God, and God's Law and God are not different things or facts, in the sense that an earthly king and his law are different. Because God is an Idea, Law Himself. Therefore it is impossible to conceive God as breaking the Law. He therefore does not rule our actions and withdraw Himself. When we say He rules our actions, we are simply using human language and we try to limit Him. Otherwise He and His Law abide everywhere and govern everything. Therefore I do not think that He answers in every detail every request of ours, but there is no doubt that He rules our action, and I literally believe that not a blade of grass grows or moves without His will. The free will we enjoy is less than that of a passenger on a crowded deck."

"Do you feel a sense of freedom in your communion with God?"

"I do. I do not feel cramped as I would on a boat full of passengers. Although I know that my freedom is less than that of a passenger. I appreciate that freedom as I have imbibed through and through the central teaching of the Gita that man is the maker of his own destiny in the sense that he has freedom of choice as to the manner in which he uses that freedom. But he is no controller of results. The moment he thinks he is, he comes to grief."

"Thank you."

Ramgarh, 16-3-'40 M. D.

*Harijan,* 23-3-'40

## 25

## A HOT GOSPELLER

Contact with people who have a mission and burning faith in it gives us a tonic feeling, whether we agree with them or not. And when they are octogenarians they seem to radiate energy and infuse new life into us. I have in mind, as I write this, people like the late Sir Daniel Hamilton, the present Metropolitan Bishop of India, Dr. John Mott, and Aimee Macpherson. I had the same feeling when Lady Emily Kinnaird was here the other day to deliver to Gandhiji the gospel of Christ. Lady Kinnaird belongs to a family which has done a lot for the spread of the gospel. Her mother, she proudly recounts, had two loves—Y. M. C. A. and India, and the three daughters, including Lady Emily, all unmarried, have tried to give their best to their mother's cherished objects.

Lady Emily seems to be a regular reader of *Harijan,* and though she is 86 is full of energy and enterprise. She must have known that, if she cannot change at her age, neither can Gandhiji, but evidently she gave Gandhiji credit for a more open mind—perhaps because he is younger, and he immediately addressed her as 'mother'—when she came to deliver the message of Christ to him.

She seemed to doubt the utility of Gandhiji's 'Appeal to Every Briton', but she said: 'Don't you think Denmark has carried out your ideal of non-violence?'

'Not a bit,' said Gandhiji. 'It was a surrender, and what I have asked for is not surrender, but non-violent resistance.'

'But Denmark did not resist and did exactly as you have advised Britons today!'

'But I have not asked for unresisting surrender or capitulation. I have appealed to Britons and everyone in their plight to display the highest courage that man is capable of, viz. to refuse to use arms and to defy the enemy to walk over their dead bodies. Denmark did nothing of the kind.'

'But Denmark had no time. It was all so sudden, and there was nothing for it but for her to offer no resistance.'

'I know, I know,' said Gandhiji. 'But it is such suddenness that puts non-violence to the test. It was no doubt prudent on her part to offer no resistance. But prudence is not the same thing as non-violence. Non-violent resistance is far more effective than violent resistance, and that is what I have asked for from these nations which are so accustomed to violent resistance.'

'Well, well, what's the good of it?' said Lady Emily incredulously.

'What was the good of Jesus Christ laying down His life?' asked Gandhiji.

'Oh, that was a different matter. He was the son of God.'

'And so are we!'

'No,' protested Lady Emily. 'He was the *only* son of God.'

'It is there,' said Gandhiji, 'that the mother (she) and son (Gandhiji) must differ. With you Jesus was the only begotten son of God. With me He was a son of God, no matter how much purer than us all, but every one of us is a son of God and capable of doing what Jesus did, if we but endeavour to express the Divine in us.'

That gave Lady Emily the cue for her sermon. 'Yes, that is where I think you are wrong. If you accepted Christ in your heart and appealed to your people to do likewise, you could deliver your message with greater ease and far better effect.' I am quoting from memory, as I kept no notes of the interview. But I am sure I am not being unfair to her, as she repeated this message to me in a long interview with me two days after the interview with Gandhiji. 'He is our salvation, and without receiving Him in our hearts we cannot be saved,' she added.

'So those who accept the Christ are all saved. They need do nothing more?'

'We are sinners all,' said Lady Emily, 'and we have but to accept Him to be saved.'

'And then we may continue to be sinners? Is that what you mean?' asked Gandhiji, laughing heartily. 'You do not, I hope, belong to the Plymouth Brothers, do you?'

'No,' I am a Presbyterian.'

'But you talk like some of the Plymouth Brothers I met long ago in South Africa.'

'Yes, I am afraid you were so unfortunate in the Christian contacts you formed in South Africa. You did not meet the right kind of people.'

'Surely you will not say that. I met a number of estimable people. They were all honest and sincere.'

'But they were not *true* Christians.'

Gandhiji then gave a graphic account of his contact with a number of Christians in those early days, ending up with the intimate contact with F. W. Meyer.* 'Do you know F. W. Meyer?' he asked Lady Emily.

'Oh yes,' she said.

* For a detailed account see Part I, chapters 4 and 5, pp. 8-15.

'Well, then, let me tell you,' said Gandhiji, 'that it was F. W. Meyer who after a long talk with me asked the other Christian friends to let me alone. He said to them that I was as good as converted, and that I did not need any formal process of conversion. But of course that did not satisfy them. And old A. W. Baker, who must be much over eighty now, is still at me. He writes to remind me time and again that unless I accept Christ in his way I cannot be saved.'

Lady Emily was on the same mission as Mr. A. W. Baker, but she thought she had an entirely new. message to deliver. And no wonder. Everyone who is fired with a message must feel that every time he delivers it he has something new to say. But the very mention of Coates, Miss Gabb, Miss Harris, Spencer Walton, F. W. Meyer and others was a joy to Lady Emily. For she said with almost victorious delight: 'But you *do* think of those Christians, Mr. Gandhi, even at this distance of time!'

And she wondered why we were so obtuse as not to see what was so obvious to her—the outstanding superiority of the message of Christianity to any other message. The Bible had been translated into several hundred languages, and the heathen in the remotest parts of the world, who knew not a syllable of English, was agreeably surprised to find God's message delivered to him in his own dialect.

'That proves nothing,' said Gandhiji again laughing. Lady Emily also laughed, quite unperturbed by the fact that what she was saying was like pouring so much water over the duck's back. The very first qualification of a preacher is unperturbed serenity.

'And then,' Lady Emily added, 'whereas fifty years ago there were so many hundred thousand Christians in India, there are today ten times as many.'

'Again,' said Gandhiji, 'that proves nothing.'

'But why all this quarrel about labels?' added Gandhiji at the end of the long argument. 'Cannot a few hundred thousand Indians or Africans live the message of Christ without being called Christians?'

'No, for without the grace of Jesus one cannot be saved. One has to accept Christ in one's heart,' she maintained. 'That is the definition of a true Christian, and I admit there are very few Christians today.'

As usual with these battles, this one was a draw, and Lady Emily parted in the greatest good humour. In two days she returned to deliver the same message to me. She repeated the same argument, dwelt upon the glories of conversion, upon the great work that the Christian missionaries had done, and asked me why I missed no occasion to have a dig at the good missionaries. 'But,' said I, 'I have numerous friends amongst them, and they understand me and I understand them. As for conversion let me tell you that long before Jesus delivered His message, the prayer was offered in India by our wisest men, and it had been handed down to us for centuries: Lead us from the unreal to the Real, from darkness to Light, from death to Immortality. Our progress from the one to the other was a process of conversion.'

'But whenever I talk with you people,' said Lady Emily, 'you talk of centuries ago, but do not talk of today.'

'When you talk of true Christianity you too have to go back 1900 years, and if we have belied the message of our great teachers, so have you. What can be a greater betrayal of Christianity than the present war?' I rejoined.

'But those who have betrayed it are not true Christians.'

'Well, then, Lady Emily, I would say it would be far better for you to address your message to those who calling themselves Christians are betraying Christ's message than to those who do not profess to be Christians. For their life is a greater insult to Christianity than those of non-Christians.'

I think Lady Emily saw the point, for she said, 'When we came to India we came to reconvert the English missionaries. That was our sole mission.'

'I wish you kept that your sole mission even today.'

'But you are trying to judge us,' said Lady Emily, slightly hurt perhaps. 'Do not judge. Do you remember the verse—"Except ye be born again"? We have to be born again.'

'Yes, I remember the verse. See that Bible on my bookshelf. For I hold it in the same respect as I do my Bhagavadgita. But the text means to me nothing more than the Upanishad text I gave you a moment ago. I am not trying to judge you. I am judging myself too. We are all being judged today, and we have all to be born again from untruth to Truth, from darkness to Light, from death to Immortality.'

I have summarized very briefly a long argument. But though again the argument was a draw, to talk with that doughty champion was an exhilarating experience.

Sevagram, 27-7-'40 M. D.

*Harijan*, 4-8-'40

## 26

## INDIA'S MESSAGE

There was an extra rush of visitors and interviewers to see Gandhiji during the last week of the dying year. A group of earnest young American teachers from Ewing College and the Agricultural Institute, Allahabad, who were returning to America and paid Gandhiji a visit, asked him, "How would you, an old and experienced leader, advise young men to throw away their lives in the service of humanity?"

"The question is not rightly put," replied Gandhiji. "You don't throw away your lives when you take up the weapon of Satyagraha. But you prepare yourselves to face without retaliation the gravest danger and provocation. It gives you a chance to surrender your life for the cause when the time comes. To be able to do so non-violently requires previous training. If you are a believer in the orthodox method, you go and train yourselves as soldiers. It is the same with non-violence. You have to alter your whole mode of life and work for it in peace time just as much as in the time of war. It is no doubt a difficult job. You have to put your whole soul into it; and if you are sincere, your example will affect the lives of other people around you. America is today exploiting the so-called weaker nations of the world along with other powers. It has become the richest country in the world, not a thing to be proud of, when we come to think of the means by which she has become rich. Again, to protect these riches you need the assistance of violence. You must be prepared to give up these riches. Therefore, if you really mean to give up violence, you will say, "We shall have nothing to do with the spoils of violence, and if as a result America ceases to be rich, we do not mind." You will then be qualified to offer a spotless sacrifice. That is the meaning of preparation. The occasion for making the extreme sacrifice may not come if you as a nation have fully learnt to live for peace. It is much more difficult to live for non-violence than to die for it."

The friends wanted to know if non-violence as enunciated by Gandhiji has a positive quality. "If I had used the word 'love', which non-violence is in essence, you would not have asked this question," replied Gandhiji. "But perhaps 'love' does not express my meaning fully. The nearest word is 'charity'. We love our friends and our equals. But the reaction that a ruthless dictator sets up in us is either that of awe or pity according respectively as we react to him violently or non-violently. Non-violence knows no fear. If I am truly non-violent, I would pity the dictator and say to myself, "He does not know what a human being should be. One day he will know better when he is confronted by a people who do not stand in awe of him, who will neither submit nor cringe to him, nor bear any grudge against him for whatever he may do. Germans are today doing what they are doing because all the other nations stand in awe of them. None of them can go to Hitler with clean hands."

"What is the place of Christian missions in the new India that is being built up today? What can they do to help in this great task?"

"To show appreciation of what India is and is doing," replied Gandhiji. "Up till now they have come as teachers and preachers with queer notions about India and India's great religions. We have been described as a nation of superstitious heathens, knowing nothing, denying God. We are a brood of Satan as Murdoch would say. Did not Bishop Heber in his well-known hymn "From Greenland's icy mountains" describe India as a country where "every prospect pleases and only man is vile"? To me this is a negation of the spirit of Christ. My personal view, therefore, is that, if you feel that India has a message to give to the world, that India's religions too are true, though like all religions imperfect for having percolated through imperfect human agency, and you come as fellow-helpers and fellow-seekers, there is a place for you here. But if you come as preachers of the 'true gospel' to a people who are wandering in darkness, so far as I am concerned you can have no place. You may impose yourselves upon us."

This provoked the question, "What is India's real message to the world?"

"Non-violence," replied Gandhiji. "India is saturated with that spirit. It has not demonstrated it to the extent that you can go to America as living witnesses of that spirit. But you can truthfully say that India is making a desperate effort to live up to that great ideal. If there is not this message, there is no other message that India can give. Say what you may, the fact stands out that here you have a whole sub-continent that has decided for itself that there is no freedom for it except through non-violence. No other country has made that attempt even. I have not been able to influence other people even to the extent of believing that non-violence is worth trying. There is of course a growing body of European opinion that has begun to appreciate the possibilities of the weapon of non-violence. But I want the sympathy of the whole world for India if she can get it while she is making this unique experiment. You can, however, be witnesses to the attempt only if you really feel that we are making an honest effort to come up to the ideal of non-violence and that all we are doing is not fraud. If your conviction is enlightened and deep enough, it will set up a ferment working in the minds of your people."

"This is an admirable charge," commented one of the friends.

"Take that charge with you then," replied Gandhiji.

Segaon, 29-12-'38 PYARELAL

*Harijan*, 7-1-'39

## 27

## A TALK WITH CHRISTIAN FRIENDS

In an essay the Very Reverend Dean Inge wrote during the last war, he showed that the founder of the Christian religion had a horror of labels. He cared nothing whether a man was a Jew or a Samaritan, Roman or Greek. He did not exalt *ipso facto* those who said "Lord, Lord" above the Scribes and Pharisees. He founded no Church. "The maxim *Extra ecclesiamnulla salus* (Outside the Church there is no salvation)," observed the Dean, "is the most un-Christian of all doctrines, except *Melius est ut unus pereat quan unitas* (It is better that one man perish than unity)." I was forcefully reminded of these remarks of the Reverend Dean as I listened to the arguments of some Christian friends who visited Sevagram during the first week of this month. One of them, a professor from the South, was developing before Gandhiji the case for conversion from a Christian missionary's standpoint. "As a Christian," he began, "I believe that God Himself entered the world in the form of Jesus Christ. I place Jesus Christ in the position of God-man. He differs from all other prophets not in degree only but in kind. He is God incarnate and the only incarnation of God." "I know," he proceeded, "Hindus and Muslims, so long as they are Hindus and Muslims, cannot share this position. But as a servant of Jesus Christ and his gospel I can hold no other. The Christ founded a visible organic society on earth, not merely an invisible bond of union in sacrament. I claim the right to preach the truth of Jesus Christ by word and life. I must pray that the hearts of all people may behold in Jesus God incarnate and be led to enter His visible Church. And so the Christians strive and labour to that end. This right of propagation of the gospel is part of our religious freedom. Will you under

Swaraj allow Christians to go on with their proselytizing activity without any hindrance?" He paused for a reply.

"No legal hindrance," replied Gandhiji, "can be put in the way of any Christian or of anybody preaching for the acceptance of his doctrine."

The visitor was anxious to know whether the freedom they were having under the British regime would be allowed them under the national Government without any interference.

"I can't answer that question categorically," replied Gandhiji, "because I do not know what is exactly allowed and what is not allowed under the British regime today. That is a legal question. Besides, what is permitted may not necessarily be the same thing as what is *permissible* under the law. All, therefore, I can say is that you should enjoy all the freedom you are entitled to under the law today."

Gandhiji's visitor said, "Our position is that, holding the viewpoint that we do, we cannot give up our mission work as we are today carrying it out, even under persecution. Some of us are under an apprehension that they may have hereafter to labour under such disabilities. Is there any guarantee that such a thing would not happen?"

"As I wrote in *Harijan*," replied Gandhiji, "you do not seem to realize that Christians are today enjoying privileges because they are Christians. The moment a person here turns Christian, he becomes a *Saheb log*. He almost changes his nationality. He gets a job and position which he could not have otherwise got. He adopts foreign dress and ways of living. He cuts himself off from his own people and begins to fancy himself a limb of the ruling class. What the Christians are afraid of losing, therefore, is not their rights but anomalous privileges."

The visitor admitted the truth of Gandhiji's remarks, but assured him that whatever might have been the case in the past, Christians as a class no longer wished to retain any exceptional privileges.

Another missionary friend recalling Gandhiji's well-known objection to the prevailing proselytizing practices chimed in: "Why may not I share with others my experience of Jesus Christ which has given me such an ineffable peace?"

"Because," replied Gandhiji, "you cannot possibly say that what is best for you is best for all. Quinine may be the only means of saving life in your case, but a dangerous poison in the case of another. And again, is it not super-arrogation to assume that you alone possess the key to spiritual joy and peace, and that an adherent of a different faith cannot get the same in equal measure from a study of his scriptures? I enjoy a peace and equanimity of spirit which has excited the envy of many Christian friends. I have got it principally through the Gita.

"Your difficulty lies in your considering the other faiths as false or so adulterated as to amount to falsity. And you shut your eyes to the truth that shines in the other faiths and which gives equal joy and peace to their votaries. I have not hesitated, therefore, to recommend to my Christian friends a prayerful and sympathetic study of the other scriptures of the world. I can give my own humble testimony that, whilst such study has enabled me to give the same respect to them that I give to my own, it has enriched my own faith and broadened my vision."

Gandhiji's interlocutor was silent. "What would be your message to a Christian like me and my fellows?" the professor finally asked. Gandhiji replied, "Become worthy of the message that is imbedded in the Sermon on the Mount, and join the spinning brigade."

I have epitomized a fairly long conversation and given only those parts which were of topical interest.

Sevagram, 6-1-'40 PYARELAL

*Harijan*, 13-1-'40

## 28

## A GOOD SAMARITAN

Dr. Chesterman, the medical secretary of the English Baptist Mission started by Carey, has had four and half months in India. He came out to attend the Tambaram Conference as well as to visit as many of the mission hospital centres as he could, for whose interests he is responsible in London. He was anxious to have an interview with Gandhiji before sailing for England on the 18th and came to Sevagram on the 13th.

He began by expressing his gratitude to Gandhiji for the privilege afforded to him in spite of Gandhiji's ill-health of which he, as a medical man, appreciated the serious nature. He said he had been overwhelmed with the perplexity of Indian problems, and naturally the medical ones had taken first place in his mind. When he heard that 2 lakhs of women die yearly from child-birth, 1 lakh from small pox, 36 lakhs from indiscriminate fevers, that there are 10 lakhs of lepers and 6 lakhs of blind persons, he confessed he was appalled with the immensity of the task of both preventive and curative medicine. He was not sure whether Gandhiji was aware of the fact that there were 266 mission hospitals and 500 dispensaries in India, 254 European and 350 Indian doctors, 300 European and 800 Indian nurses, 2 million patients seen and 5 million treated per annum in these hospitals, that half of the T. B. work and almost the entire work of lepers was in the hands of missions. While, of course, the work of conversion was there and he knew Gandhiji's opinion on this subject, he wanted to draw attention to the fact that three-quarters of their medical work lay in areas where there was no response to religious teaching. Dr. Chesterman said very feelingly that he would like to know that medical missions were agents of goodwill from their side, especially at a time when tension and racial bitterness were great, that they would love to be moved, as Christ was, with compassion and thereby vindicate God's goodness. He would, therefore, much like to have Gandhiji's opinion on how the work could be most fruitfully developed and how far they could count on support and co-operation.

In reply Gandhiji said that the answer was difficult and yet simple at the same time. "I hold peculiar views on the function of medicine. I expressed these very forcibly years ago, and nothing in all the course of my long experience since has made me change them in essence. But there is no need for me to expound these to you now. I have visited many mission hospitals, seen the wonderful work of the missionaries among lepers. This work may be called their monopoly and speciality, for practically no one else has come in to take it up. I know the Leper Home in Cuttack. I have spent quite a long time in the Purulia Leper Asylum and been very struck with the work there. Then I have seen Mrs. Higginbotham's work in Allahabad and several other places too, for I love to visit leper homes. But in spite of all this admiration of mine for the work of medical missionaries there has always been a mental reservation and criticism within me. I have felt that these good and well-intentioned missionaries have not touched the fringe of the question. Certainly good work has been done for lepers, for the blind, for sufferers from T. B. and other ailments, but the help has not really touched the suffering millions of this great land. Medical aid has been made available in the main to those who live in or near the cities—whereas the bulk of India's population in our villages has been untouched. Provincial Governments, even Congress Governments, are appalled at the need of the villager. They do not know what to do, and nothing great has yet been done in spite of various experiments. Therefore, if I were asked to advise missionaries or Mission Boards, I would ask them not to try to transplant the entire system of Western medicine into India. We cannot afford it. There is ever so much to be gleaned and had from the study of indigenous drugs and medicines, but practically very little work has been done in this department. No one has made it his business to go out into our fields and search, and much of the indigenous talent, simply because it is not considered original or scientific, is running to waste. I will give you an incident which happened only today. As you may know I have had a little swelling on one foot for some days now which has alarmed the doctors because they feel that it is a sign denoting the commencing disintegration of the heart and kidneys. One of my co-workers here—you may call him almost an illiterate man—was very troubled, as all are, about me and tells me he could not sleep last night. This morning he brought me a green leaf and told me that it had cured his father of the same trouble and begged of me to try it also. I had no hesitation in acceding to his proposal—whereas, if I had had a bewildering prescription given me by a highly qualified doctor, my reaction would not have been the same. I feel, therefore, that in these simple ways lies relief for the villager. I do not say that the leaf will answer the purpose. But there should be an agency that can say with certainty what these herbs are and what is their quality." Gandhiji then went on to explain that he had no prejudice against Western medicine or doctors. He had today sent for glucose for Mr. Kallenbach, a South African friend of his who was lying ill with malaria and who was refusing to take quinine, a drug in which Gandhiji himself had implicit faith.

Here Dr. Chesterman interposed and said that quinine was an indigenous drug, to which Gandhiji replied that though that was so it was a monopoly and therefore very expensive and utterly beyond the reach of the villager. "I should therefore," he went on to say, "like to see missionaries as medicine vendors for the villages, confining themselves, as far as they can, to indigenous medicines. There will certainly not be gold medals or knighthoods from Government forthcoming for them for this valuable research work. But, in my opinion, they will obtain what is of far greater value, a knighthood from Jesus Christ." Proceeding Gandhiji said that he had felt for a long time that the medical faculty in India should manufacture a short course of training for village workers, and had told Surgeon-General Hooten of Bombay so, many years ago. Village school teachers should be utilized for this purpose. They should look upon the entire village as under their jurisdiction from the point of view of health and teach the simple laws of hygiene and prevention of disease to the inhabitants. Their schools could be used as dispensaries for the distribution of ordinary medicines for simple ailments. He gave the analogy of the useful six weeks' first aid training which he himself had had to undergo before he could form and lead the ambulance corps which he did during the Boer War.

Dr. Chesterman agreed and related how he had been working as a pioneer in the Congo for sixteen years and how he had been convinced that community service to villagers was by far the most important work for them to undertake there. It is interesting to note that today, in their working area of over 10,000 square miles, no villager has to go for more than ten or fifteen miles to procure medical aid. He fully believed in locally recruited, locally trained, and locally employed workers rather than the exotic product. In the Congo they were giving a three years' training course to African young men which fitted them to administer medicines for all simple ailments and gave them a working knowledge of simple surgery too. These workers start with a salary of Rs. 15 rising to Rs. 30 p.m. They are put in charge of dispensaries and carry on their ministry under the guidance and supervision of doctors who visit them frequently. They are not allowed any private practice.

Dr. Chesterman then asked Gandhiji his opinion on expenditure on buildings and elaborate equipment for hospitals. Gandhiji replied saying that he had always been opposed to this and was invariably trying to wean people from spending on what was unnecessary when for so much that was urgently needed money was lacking. Big hospitals did not help the poor man in the long run, for they did not educate him to understand how he ought to look after his health once he left the hospital.

The next question was: "What contribution can medical missionaries make towards the raising of ethical standards in professional life?"

Gandhiji said: "They can help, but I do not feel they can do much according to my measurement. You may think me uncharitable, but so long as the mental reservation is there that medical missionaries would like all their patients and co-workers to become converts to Christianity, so long will there remain a bar to real brotherhood. Then there is the additional handicap that they belong to the ruling race, and that is responsible for their aloofness. Missionaries have not learnt the maxim 'When you go to Rome do as Rome does.' They retain everything of the West in their daily lives forgetting that clothes and food and modes of life are in response to climate and to surroundings, and adjustment, therefore, becomes necessary. They have not stooped to conquer. The gulf of mutual distrust exists, and there is, therefore, no easy passage between the medical missionary and the medical profession in India." Dr. Chesterman disputed this statement. He maintained that there was any amount of goodwill also. He had met a Hindu friend in Bombay who had definitely assured him that there was need for mission hospitals because Indians got greater consideration and greater compassion there than in Government institutions.

Asked whether mission hospitals were justified in

taking fees from those able to afford them, unlike Government institutions where money was generally extracted by the subordinate staff in undesirable ways, Gandhiji said he saw no reason against it.

The last question Dr. Chesterman asked was whether Gandhiji's objection to conversion applied to areas like the Kond Hills where the aboriginal races were animists. The unhesitating reply was, "Yes. It does apply, because I know that in spite of being described as animists these tribes have from times immemorial been absorbed in Hinduism. They are, like the indigenous medicine, of the soil, and their roots lie deep there. But you can only endorse this if you feel that Hinduism is as true as Christianity. I hold that all religions are true but imperfect inasmuch as they are presented through human agency and bear the impress of the imperfections and frailties of the human being. My quarrel with missionaries is that they think no religion other than Christianity is true."

In parting from Gandhiji, while thanking him for the time he had given and hoping the conversation had not unduly tired him, Dr. Chesterman implored Gandhiji to continue to appeal to the best that was in them. The feeling answer that greatly touched Dr. Chesterman was, "I am making that appeal incessantly from the innermost recesses of my heart. That is of far more value than the written word although I have indulged in that also."

But Dr. Chesterman was destined to see Sevagram again. Having noted Mr. Kallenbach's serious condition and sensed Gandhiji's anxiety about him, he felt that he would like to cancel his programme of visiting Poona before sailing on the 18th and return to the village to see if he could be of any help. In Sevagram Gandhiji was about to send a wire for a specialist to help Dr. Sushila Nayar when, to the agreeable surprise of all, Dr. Chesterman turned up. As soon as he heard of his coming, Gandhiji exclaimed, "There is the visible hand of God in this. Such things have happened often enough in my life. I do not regard them as accidents."

For Dr. Chesterman it was an opportunity. Providence had afforded him of spending another 24 hours with Gandhiji and rendering service to a friend in distress. He said to the writer, "The memory of this visit will be treasured by me to my dying day." For Gandhiji it was a link between East and West.

Sevagram, 17-2-'39 AMRIT KAUR

*Harijan*, 25-2-'39

## 29

## THEIR HOPES

Among the group there were some who are nowadays known by the name of 'Christian Harijans'. The phrase is a misnomer, but it demonstrates how the canker of untouchability has travelled beyond its limits and has contaminated other faiths also. The Harijans who some time back changed their faith to escape the hardships inflicted on them by Caste Hindus have, they say, fared no better in the Christian fold. The stigma of untouchability still attaches to them. Many of them have met Gandhiji in Malabar and Tamil Nad and asked for redress of their wrongs. "We are in the same position," said the friends present at this interview, "as Adi-Dravida Hindus. Are we to have any share in this movement?"

"Indirectly, yes," said Gandhiji.

"But we do not get any benefit at all."

"You are getting indirect benefit. The Christian missionaries are wide awake and recognize that they should do something."

Lifelong suffering had made the friends impatient. They said, "We have decided to face the oppressors boldly. We think of changing our faith."

"I cannot say anything about that. But I feel that oppression can be no reason for changing one's faith."

"We have no other go. Shall we get any relief in future from this movement?"

"Yes," replied Gandhiji, "I am absolutely certain that, if this movement succeeds, untouchability in Christianity is also bound to go."

C. S.

*Harijan*, 23-2-'34

30

## 'TOWARDS THIS GRAND REALIZATION'

Ever since coming to Tamil Nad, Gandhiji had been longing to see Christukulashram, an institution 140 miles to the south-west of Madras run by Dr. S. Jesudasan and Dr. Forrestor-Paton, two Christians, the former an Indian and the latter a Scotsman—both medical men. With an aspiration to realize 'a deeper personal experience of the life in Christ and the fellowship of love and the power for service springing out of it,' they started this institution nine years back. Their report says: "We felt it (the name Ashram) expressed in a language understood by the people our oneness with them and our belief that whatever was beautiful and true in the past heritage of India should find its fulfilment and enrichment in the kingdom of God." They aspire after 'sharing in a wider fellowship', and bringing Christianity out of what they believe to be 'self-seeking isolation'. They are trying to realize that 'wider fellowship' through selfless service of the lowliest around them by giving them medical aid and elementary education. They do not baptize people. They do not decry other religions, for they profess to have a regard for them. They try to fashion their lives so as to be in consonance with their surroundings. They, therefore, wear home-spun cloth and share the national aspirations of the people. They have built a church after the model of a South Indian Hindu temple.

Expressing his delight before a small meeting of villagers coming from the neighbourhood, Gandhiji said, "It seems that I have come to one of my homes." Giving the gist of his message, he said, "It is not enough that Caste Hindus begin to touch Harijans. Mere touch can give me no satisfaction whatsoever. Their hearts must be moved, and they must sincerely believe that it is an affront to human dignity to consider a single human being as lower than one's self. In that sense you can easily understand why I call this movement against untouchability one for the realization of the brotherhood of man—not merely of Hindu man, but of man in general, no matter to what part of the world he belongs, to what race he belongs or to what faith he belongs. For Caste Hindus to change their hearts in connection with those whom they consider untouchables is merely a stepping-stone to this grand realization. I have invited the whole world to take part in this movement; and the whole world can take part in this movement by extending its sympathy to it and by studying it."

C. S.

*Harijan*, 2-3-'34

## 31

## CHRISTIANS IN INDEPENDENT INDIA

Gandhiji warned the Hindus, the Muslims and the Sikhs against entertaining any ill-will towards the Christians, who were a minority in India. Nor should they entertain any wish about converting them to Hinduism, Islam or Sikhism. He did not believe in such conversions. He wanted the Christians to be good Christians, the Muslims to be good Muslims, the Sikhs to be good Sikhs, and the Hindus to be good Hindus under all circumstances. That to him was real conversion.

He had seen in the papers that in view of the fact that State patronage to Christianity or any other religion would not be given, 75% of the churches in India would have to be closed down. Gandhiji said that religion could never be served through money. The Christians should rejoice that an artificial prop was being removed. God was omnipresent. Our bodies were the real temples rather than buildings of stone. The best place for congregational worship for any religion in his opinion was in the open with the sky above as the canopy and mother earth below for the floor. Every individual was the protector of his own religion against the whole world.

[A Post-Prayer Speech]

Delhi, 24-12-'47
*Harijan*, 4-1-'48

# INDEX